SCENES FROM THE PAST : 29

WOODHEAD

---- PART ONE ----

MANCHESTER LONDON ROAD GORTON, GUIDE BRIDGE, GLOSSOP and the LONGDENDALE VALLEY

AF859523

Godley East Junction, February 8th.1952: The Woodhead route was one of stark contrasts. The western side, out from Manchester, passed at one time through some of the most heavily industrialised suburbs of any city in the country. Beyond the Cheshire market town of Hyde, though, more open vistas were encountered as the railway continued a steady uphill climb towards the line's summit at Woodhead. Godley East Junction saw the end of loop lines from nearby Godley Junction where large quantities of freight, the line's lifeblood, were exchanged from adjoining CLC territory. Here is a scene so typical of the route's traffic over the years: Class 04/8 No.**63853** slogs eastwards with a train of coal empties under the electric catenary which would later transform the line. The massive structure overhead is known locally as "Hattersley Viaduct" and was the subject of extensive civil engineering works which will be referred to in the book. *Tom Lewis*

Book Law Publications
Nottingham

E.M.JOHNSON

COPYRIGHT @ E M JOHNSON 2012
ISBN 978-1-907094-88-0

ALL RIGHTS RESERVED

FIRST PUBLISHED 1996
REPRINTED 1998, 2006, 2012

PRINTED BY THE AMADEUS PRESS
CLECKHEATON BD19 4TQ

PUBLISHED BY
BOOK LAW PUBLICATIONS
382 CARLTON HILL
NOTTINGHAM NG4 1JA

DEDICATION I take great pleasure in repeating the dedication of this re-printed volume of part one of the Woodhead line to my dear and loving wife Mary. To attempt to render adequate thanks for all she has done in the years I have been writing is difficult. Parts of our home are perpetually flooded with what, I am sure, must seem like an endless sea of maps, paperwork and photographs. Cheerfully, willingly and ever uncomplainingly, Mary supports me in all I do, her work and dedication being vital to my tasks. What more could any husband and writer ask?

WOODHEAD

- PART ONE -

MANCHESTER LONDON ROAD GORTON GUIDE BRIDGE GLOSSOP AND THE LONGDENDALE VALLEY

(Above) Manchester London Road. It is twenty minutes to five in the afternoon and all the hustle and bustle of edwardian Manchester is seen around London Road station approach in this view from the corner of Auburn Street. The date of the photograph is unknown but almost certainly post-1901, determined by the presence of electric tram-cars albeit still of the open top variety. The motor car has yet to make its presence felt and it will be a generation or more before the horse drawn cabs relinquish their hold on passenger trade. To the left is the capacious goods station of the London & North Western Railway Company, backdrop to the proliferation of advertising hoardings.Facilities for the Great Central were behind and fronted onto Ducie Street. The station building, designed by architects Mills and Murgatroyd, replaced the earlier Store Street station which has at times been referred to by some sources as 'Bank Top'. ***Authors collection***

From early beginnings in Travis Street, the station on London Road was enlarged by degrees in the latter part of the nineteenth century as rail-borne traffic grew and grew. The LNWR and MS&L, never the happiest of partners, were required, via the London Road Station Act of 1859, to put their respective houses in order and manage the running of the station under the aegis of a General Superintendent. A further Act (Enlargement & Regulation of Manchester London Road Station) dated June 12th 1861, gave the MS&L powers to use *"two new lines of rails-which will be appropriated to them for all purposes of their traffic."* For this privilege they were required to to pay the LNWR an annual rent of £350.00 plus various tolls for each movement in and out of the station. Tolls ranged from 1d for a First Class passenger to one farthing for a double journey for an "excursionist". Dogs were charged one halfpenny, horses two-pence and goods and minerals were levied at $1\frac{6}{10}$ of a penny per ton.

Under a later Act, dated June 17th 1898, the LNWR were given powers to widen their line between London Road station and Ardwick. it is this last piece of legislation that reminds us of London Road's history and the MS&L's part in it. Under this last Act a new pair of running lines were built on the north side (*above North Western Street*) of the existing formation. These were then given over to the (by now) Great Central; the latter, in turn, handed back to the LNWR the two lines in use previously for its traffic.

Foreword

Ardwick Station, March 7th.1957: The long, low and curving Up platform at Ardwick Station viewed from the cab of Co-Co Electric No.**27003** en route from Manchester to Leicester via Sheffield Victoria. It was from the spot immediately below the catenary support that my youthful observations of Electric "boxes" at speed were made at the time this picture was taken. The tracks on the right are those of the LMR lines in and out of London Road station via Longsight. It was from Ardwick that the erstwhile SA&M and M&B railways shared a common path into the original station at Travis Street. Ardwick No.1 signalbox sits in the background in the fork between the two sets of tracks. The entry to Bennett's sidings dips down in front of the signalbox. *B.K.B.Green*

The discipline and rigour at St.Gregory's School Ardwick, Manchester was of the nature that would, today, have raised calls for the institution of a Public Enquiry-such was the institutionalised violence that punctuated the everday goings-on. The buildings, constructed for what the Victorians termed a "Reform School" were, as a matter of obvious consequence, harsh, cold and uninviting. Standing around the perimeter of this educational nirvana were the bombed-out remains of a gymnasium and a classroom block, a reminder of the damage the school had suffered at the hands of the Luftwaffe in the 1939-45 war. Many of the youthful incumbents, myself included, were inclined to think that the German war machine might have had a bit more luck, though their obvious target had been the approaches to Manchester's London Road Station, within which the school was both in sight and sound of. Any relief from St.Gregory's, however slight, was always welcome and within a very short space of arriving for my five years incarceration there, I quickly found lunchtime solace on the platforms of nearby Ardwick Station. Ardwick had staggered platforms and we schoolboy enthusiasts found the best view by far of the trains entering and leaving London Road was to be had from the western end of the Up platform. This was sited at a rather unusually low angle and gave us the double advantage of a broad view of London Midland trains heading to and from Longsight and a superb, head-on spectrum of the Bo-Bo and Co-Co Electrics which, having picked speed up very quickly out of London Road, came with what always seemed lightning speed round the gentle bend in the direction of Ashburys and Gorton.

Sited just beyond the end of the platforms at Ardwick was another railway which came jutting in from the right on a brick-built viaduct near to a public house latterly called the Steam Engine Tavern. I recollect never seeing one solitary train on this railway and often wondered where it went to and what its purpose was. A serious study of the broader aspects of railways hadn't entered my consciousness in those days; I was to find out later that this was the former Lancashire & Yorkshire Railway's branch from Ardwick towards Midland Junction, Philips Park and Miles Platting. Known as "The Lanky Branch" to the signalmen at London Road it most certainly was infrequently used and has, though only fairly recently, been severed. Paradoxically, very few people seemed to have known of its existence for, when the Eastlands stadium was mooted in the Beswick area, there was a suggestion that rail access could be made available!

Our lunchtime gazes over the Ardwick railway scene were frequently punctuated by the distant rumblings of an approaching train headed by what appeared at first sight to be a square, box-like object, seemingly sprouting two eyes at the front. Bristling round that subtle bend, a swishing, feintly whining sound ensued as the locomtive tore past followed by a rake of main line coaches. This passing spectre obliterated, though for only a bare half minute or so, our view of the London Midland tracks across by Ardwick Junction signalbox. Here, things more important passed our way. For, on reflection, I think we thought of the electrically-hauled expresses as something rather sub-normal. Yes, they were alright, but I'm not sure we took their numbers down and the seven Co-Cos (then Class EM2) did not, at that time, carry names. Possibly, such embellishments might have enhanced our perception of these "boxes". Our final quarry during these lunchtime spotting sessions was the sight of the 9.45 am. express from London Euston to Manchester London Road. This was due into the terminal at 1.20 p.m. and could just be seen before the witching hour approached and we had to beat a hasty retreat along Higher Ardwick for an afternoon's further enlightenment. If this train was late, though, a hasty abandonment was made; tardiness for lessons, along with a host of other misdemeanours was not treated lightly at St.Gregory's.

Such, then, was the perception of the railway from Manchester to Sheffield of an 11-year old schoolboy. Eight years or so on, the purchase of a the second part of George Dow's celebrated "Great Central " trilogy helped to awaken a serious interest in railways and a particular interest in one company which has remained undiminished ever since.I hope this literary effort of mine will not be taken as just "another book on the Woodhead Line." Though several such works have appeared over the years, I would like to think that mine is different and offers a somewhat fresh approach. If readers agree, then this will be some reward for studying and writing about the Great Central, its antecedants and successors. And that can only be a labour of love.

E.M.Johnson. Burnage, Manchester. August 1996

Manchester London Road, September 26th.1890: Parker Class 2 No.**563** awaits departure with the 10.00 a.m. Up express. At this period the MS&L possessed four platform faces at London Road, extra accommodation having been provided in 1876. No.563 is standing at the departure platform; four roads separate the train from the photographer, who stands on one of the arrival platforms, an island affair with one other platform-serving just one road-behind. This platform layout survived until the station was rebuilt in the late 1950s. The MS&L's ownership is proclaimed for all to see and a range of contemporary advertisements set the scene: Russell's Watches, Field's Candles and the omnipresent Epps's Cocoa. "What'll Win?" asks the hoarding displaying the virtues of the Sporting Chronicle-a daily newspaper for just 1d. The striking thing about this picture is that, despite the extensive rebuilding of the late 1950s, the station is instantly recognisable to today's traveller who gazes on the same roof and side walls as our predecessors of over 100 years ago.*Collection of Jack Braithwaite*

THE RAILWAY FROM MANCHESTER TO SHEFFIELD

(The Woodhead Line)

In these days of mass transport, when Continental Europe, the Greek islands, the vast land mass of Australia and even the far-flung North and South islands of New Zealand have become holiday destinations, it hardly seems possible that travel between two northern cities, little more than 40 miles or so distant and each of major importance in burgeoning Victorian capitalist society, could have been regarded as something of an adventure taking some two days to accomplish.

Manchester had been in the very forefront of railway development:witness the opening of the Liverpool and Manchester line in 1830, followed closely by connections to Birmingham and then London, via the Lancashire town of Warrington. Thus was enabled a rail journey, albeit a somewhat tedious one, to be made between the commercial centre of the country's cotton industry and its Capital city.

As early as 1831 an Act had been obtained for the construction of a railway between Manchester and Sheffield. This was the Sheffield and Manchester Railway; the Bill received the Royal Assent on August 23rd.1831 and had capital fixed at £530,000 with associated borrowing set up to £176,000.

The route for the line had been proposed by none other than George Stephenson. Stephenson's route originated from the Liverpool and Manchester Railway on the West side of Water Street in the city and would have proceeded on a steady gradient of 1-in-792 for the seven miles or so to Stockport. From the Cheshire market town the Rivers Tame and Mersey were to be bridged before the alignment proceeded up the Goyt Valley to the vicinity of Whaley Bridge. The Goyt itself was to be bridged in various places and from Whaley Bridge a rising gradient of 1-in-81 was to be set before the line reached an obscure place called Corn Heys about a mile or so beyond Chapel Milton.

Rushop Edge, a ridge of hills, was to be the summit point for this projected Manchester to Sheffield line. Stephenson proposed to attack the face of this by means of two inclined planes: one set at a mile at 1-in-18 and a second, which was to be inside a tunnel, was to be around 1-in-32 and around three-quarters of a mile in length. There followed then a level stretch of about 1¼ miles before the descent into the Hope Valley via two more inclined planes on the common gradient of 1-in-18.

With typical Victorian ingenuity Stephenson had proposed to overcome the steepness of his inclined planes by a combination of stationary engines and a counterbalancing system of loaded limestone waggons; noting to his committee that the eastern side of the Rushop Edge was comprised of an inexhaustible (sic) store of limestone of excellent quality. A system of Scotches was proposed by Stephenson to ensure the safe passage of passengers up and down his inclined planes. To further allay fears of passenger safety, Stephenson proposed a system of braking that could be worked not just by the train "attendants" but by the passengers themselves!

On the eastern side of Rushop Edge, the proposed railway would descend at around 1-in-177 for 3½ miles. A following section would include some 3 miles in a tunnel at Hathersage. Further descent on an inclined plane at 1-in-32 would then occur on which waggons loaded with lime would act as counterweights to assist ascending trains of passengers. A further descent at 1-in-98 over a distance of 5½ miles would complete the journey into Sheffield itself.

Despite Stephenson's success with locomotives on the Liverpool and Manchester Railway and the overall esteem in which he was held, the use of rope-worked trains up and down steep inclines and reliance on brakes that could be worked by passengers, was too much to take. Henry Sanderson, a Sheffield land surveyor and a champion of railway travel between the two great cities, had criticised Stephenson's scheme in a series of pamphlets issued to the shareholders of the Sheffield and Manchester company. Though at the time, Sanderson's opposition to Stephenson's scheme must have seemed like so much heresy, it is to this relatively obscure figure that the conception of what became known as the "Woodhead Route" and with it the seed that was sown to become eventually the Great Central Railway, is owed.

Sanderson, a Sheffield man, had planned his route in the opposite direction to Stephenson: i.e. westwards out of Sheffield along the Don Valley towards Deepcar, through the vale of Midhope by Langsett and Swinden. The Pennine summit was to be surmounted at Salter's Brook. Shades of Stephenson's ideas were to be used here, for Sanderson planned inclined planes either side of the summit with trains hauled up by stationary engines. With great foresight, though, he had reckoned that the engines could be done away with if a tunnel, some two miles in length, were driven through the ridge. Having surmounted the Pennines, the easterly route to Manchester would go via Hadfield, Mottram, Godley and Stockport. A prophet indeed.

A particular flaw in Stephenson's plans had been his costing of the tunnel at Hathersage. With arguments more typical of a lawyer than a surveyor, Sanderson's coup de grace to the original scheme came when he published an estimate that the three mile tunnel would cost £97,000 as against Stephenson's estimate of £55,000. The abandonment of Stephenson's route was formally made at a meeting on June 5th.1833. Finally strangled, as George Dow has put it, "by the ropes of its inclines." It was left to the Midland Railway, some half a century later, to explore the Hope Valley.

Despite the rejection of Stephenson's scheme, the success of the Liverpool and Manchester and the almost wildfire-like spread of railways in other parts of the country, there was over 330 miles of line in existence by the end of 1835, acted as a very strong stimulus to connect the two great northern cities by rail. A provisional committee had been formed under the chairmanship of Lord Wharncliffe and

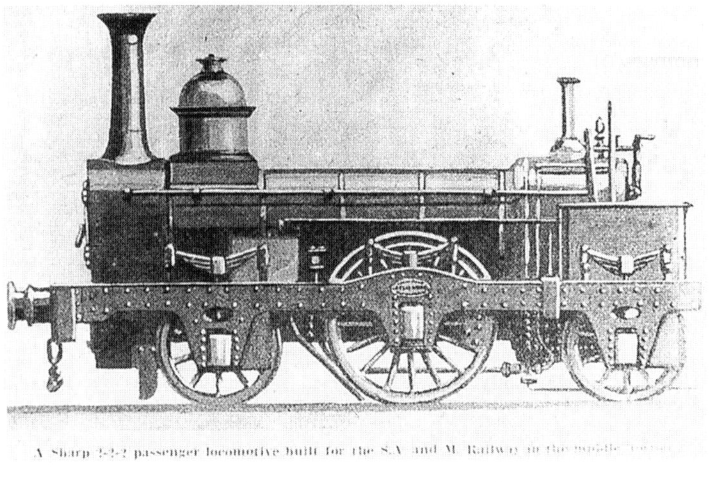

A Sharp, Roberts 2-2-2 built for the SA&M in the middle 1840s. It would have been motive power similar to this that was first used over the Woodhead line. With double frames, these engines would have burned coke. The complete absence of a cab is noteworthy. Consider that the first through journeys over the line were made in December! *Author's collection*

consisted of influential men from Sheffield, Manchester, Ashton-under-Lyne and Stalybridge. Their names, set across the pages of the prospectus outlining their scheme, looked, it had to be said, impressive. Their railway was entitled "The Sheffield, Ashton-under-Lyne and Manchester Railway." (S.AuL.&M.)

Using what appears to us today as flowery language, the prospectus set out to describe the advantages of a railway to link three great cities: "..It is needless to expatiate upon the Advantages to be derived from a Railway Communication through Districts as populous, so rich, and so important in a manufacturing point of view, as those on the projected Line; and from uniting Sheffield with the Port of Liverpool, where a very large proportion of the Manufactures of the former place are shipped, promoting and expediting as it will the intercourse between Manchester and Sheffield, and thereby increasing the general trade and business of those places, and of the several towns and villages between and thus connected with them."

Competition there was to be none. The prospectus was at pains to dismiss transport over the existing Turnpike by waggon as taking some forty hours, adding that ".....there is not the most remote probability of any competition by Water." The Railway would have it all: Capital of the company was fixed at £800,000 set in 8,000 shares of £100 each.

The services of Charles Vignoles, a prominent civil engineer of the day, along with Joseph Locke, who was Engineer on the Grand Junction Railway were secured. Vignoles had already undertaken a survey of the line and it appears that there were some differences between himself and Locke as to which would be the best route. The differences were reconciled under Lord Wharncliffe and a final report was made in November 1836. The company's capital was now confirmed at £1 million and, clearly, the railway was going places.

Vignoles had proposed a branch to Stalybridge splitting from the main line at Ashton-under-Lyne. A later proposal used a longer branch, the diverging point now being Guide Bridge instead. The main thrust of the route was via the Don and Etherow Valleys; a tunnel at the line's summit was now to be three miles in length, not two as previously proposed. Beginning at Store Street in Manchester, the line would be 40¾ miles long and would terminate east of the Cattle Market in Sheffield. Using the longer tunnel, the maximum gradient would be 1-in-120.

To allay fears about travelling through the long tunnel under the Pennines, Vignoles stated that lamps would "be affixed" and that "....the trains need only be in the tunnel for ten minutes." It is interesting to reflect that, today, over one and a half centuries later, with technology light years ahead of that available to Vignoles, there are people who fear travelling through another railway tunnel, recently opened and linking two countries!

Joseph Locke, who was to succeed Vignoles as the Railway's Engineer, waxed lyrical of the advantages of having direct communication between the eastern and western seaboards and the linking of great coalfields, the grain fields of Lincolnshire and the yarns and factories around Manchester.

Thus was fired the imagination of Great Victorian men; the Parliamentary Bill for the railway was lodged in November 1836 along with 117 others. Truly, the foundations of the great British Railway system were now being laid. Little opposition to the Bill was received; that from the Manchester and Birmingham company resulted in the

Manchester London Road, c.1918-22: J.G.Robinson's first essay in express passenger locomotive design was his Class 11B 4-4-0 which emerged in October 1901. Here, No.113 – a product of Vulcan Foundry and the last of the class to be built – has backed a goods van under the GC signalbox and into the loading dock situated between platform "C" and No.1. The 4-4-0s were designed to work the Manchester-Marylebone expresses, duties they performed until the arrival of the Atlantics and the first "Directors". Robinson appeared dissatisfied with these initial creations and quickly rebuilt two with enlarged boilers and fireboxes, these becoming Class 11C. A further variant then appeared, this time with a firebox of reduced size – Class 11D. A final development of the class saw the locomotives fitted with piston valves and superheater boilers. No.113 exchanged boilers with No.110, named *King George V,* in August 1918 at which point it received piston valves and in which condition it is seen here. The 11Bs all became LNER D9 and twenty five lasted into BR days. No.113 ended its days at March and was withdrawn in June 1939. *P.F.Cooke*

SAuL&M being given joint use of the ¾ of a mile of railway from Ardwick into what would eventually become a joint terminus at London Road, just outside of the centre of the city of Manchester.
"Cutting the sod" is a phrase buried now for long enough in railway folklore. Along with ceremonies such as laying of foundation stones for public buildings and "topping out" ceremonies for tall structures, such occasions mark the birth of great human endeavours. So it was on Monday, October 1st.1838 at 1.45 p.m. that Lord Wharncliffe, along with two of his sons, Vignoles, the Directors of the SAuL&M and their ladies, arrived on a spot of desolate moorland, near to what was to become the western entrance to the Woodhead Tunnel and close by the middle of the railway. Lord Wharncliffe cut the first sod, Vignoles did his bit, followed in turn by the company's directors. It is reported that the ladies watched the proceedings with some amusement from a nearby knoll: no doubt a combination of Victorian social custom and protocol, not to say the encumbrance of contemporary female attire, prevented them from traversing the surrounding rough ground to accompany their menfolk.
By the Spring of the following year, the entire stretch of railway had been set out all the way from Manchester to Sheffield. Charles Vignoles, who had now been appointed as Engineer-in-Chief, had come under something of a cloud-partly because of his tardy deposition of detailed reports on the line's progress. Joseph Locke of Grand Junction fame, who had vied with Vignoles on the planning of the original route, had now been requested to take over as Engineer-in-Chief. At a starting salary of £750 per annum, Locke was given responsibility for the entire execution of works: when work extended beyond the Woodhead Tunnel, his salary would rise by £250 a year.
Better progress was now being made on the line. Money was being spent in a grand fashion: three contracts had been let, taking the line from Manchester as far as Hattersley and Gamesley-a distance of some seven miles out from Manchester. In early 1841 it was announced that the new line would open for traffic as far as Godley Toll Bar-just over eight miles- in the coming September. March 1st.that year saw the opening of Summit Tunnel on the Manchester and Leeds Railway and some SAuL&M shareholders were becoming irate at seeing the possibility of a journey between Manchester and Sheffield made available via Normanton and Masborough. This, although an extremely tedious route and taking up to eight hours for a journey, was, nevertheless, viewed as de facto opposition.
In the meantime, things were proceeding apace. A number of staff had been appointed to run the new railway: these ranged from a Superintendent for the station at the Manchester end at £100 per annum down to labourers and carriage cleaners at 3/6d and 3/- per day respectively. Perhaps one of the most famous appointments to be made on the embryo line was that of "Engine Driver No.1" This was Richard Peacock who would be given control of the Locomotive Department and, in 1854, along with Charles Beyer, founded the world-famous company of Beyer, Peacock & Co. Ltd.
The projected opening to Godley Toll Bar was made, without any fuss or ceremony, on Wednesday, November 17th.1841. A trial trip had been made by the Chairman, Locke and Directors the previous Thursday. All were no doubt relieved when the Inspector of Railways, Sir.F.Smith, sanctioned the line for use by the public.
So the first public train on the SAuL&M set out from Godley at 8.00 a.m. on November 17th., that from Manchester left at 8.47 a.m. Use was made of the temporary Manchester & Birmingham terminal in Travis Street: the joint station at Store Street not being ready for use at this time. Sparse structures, made from wood, were provided at the original stations. Leaving Manchester, these were at Fairfield, Ashton and Hooley Hill which became plain "Ashton" and eventually "Guide Bridge", Dukinfield (which had the quaintly tag of "Dog Lane"), Newton and Hyde and finally, Godley Toll Bar itself.
Having ventured thus far, Locke and the Directors faced an uphill task (literally) from thereon. Two viaducts, over the Etherow at Broadbottom and at Dinting Vale, had to be erected whilst further on,

the frightful prospect of a 5,300 yard tunnel through Pennine millstone grit at Woodhead lay to be contemplated.

These were unhappy times for the SAuL&M management. Chartist troubles-a popular working-class movement that was to bring Britain almost to the point of a revolution-shareholders who dodged their calls to pay, and a nationwide depression in trade, all were heaped around to confound matters. The line to Godley, single track at first, was augmented by the opening of a passing loop at Ashton & Hooley Hill. Early in 1842 Alfred Jee, the resident engineer, was given instructions to double the railway between Fairfield and Newton & Hyde stations: the rest of the track was doubled, including the extension from Godley to Glossop (re-named Dinting when the short branch into the town was opened in 1845).

The viaduct over the River Etherow at Mottram consisted of three laminated timber arches set upon stone piers. It had been designed by Joseph Locke, but the detailed plans were drawn up by Alfred Jee. Timber construction had been used on viaducts on the Newcastle and North Shields Railway and these had been seen in a favourable light by two of the SA&M's Directors James Rhodes and George Sidebottom in the company of Charles Vignoles. It is recorded that the structure devoured 186,00 cu. ft. of stone which had been quarried from neighbouring Tintwistle. The viaduct was 506 feet long and measured 136 feet high from bottom to top.

Carrying the railway over Dinting Vale, and of much longer proprtions, was the Dinting Viaduct. This consisted of five main timber arches, each of 125 feet span set inside eleven brick approach arches: seven on one side, four on the other. The timber used was of a type known as Memel (a type of Baltic fir); some 40,000 cu. feet being required. The ribs were 4'-6" deep by 18 ins. wide and comprised 3" thick planks fastened together every 4 feet with oak trenails. The timber decking was supported off the ribs by solid timber struts. When complete, the timber structure was treated with copper sulphate to act as a preservative.

An interesting personal sidelight on the Dinting viaduct occured in October 1990 when I had the pleasure of meeting a lively 88-year old, Mr.Charles Brophy of The Ashes, just outside Glossop. A delightful character, Charlie began work on the Great Central in 1918 and retired as a Driver in 1967. He recalled to me how his Great Grandfather, an Irish ship builder, had been recruited by Buxton and Clarke, contractors, to come over to England and work on the viaduct. His ancestor had settled in Dinting and married a local girl who worked as a weaver. Charlie was, at one time, based at Dinting shed and was the last of his generation who had both lived and worked in the area. He died in July 1991.

Sound though Mr.Brophy's work was, though, by the late 1850s both Dinting and Etherow viaducts had suffered quite severe deterioration. In 1859 they were inspected by William Fairbairn who reported considerable distortion and pronounced the structures to be in an unsafe condition. Fairbairn recommended that the timber spans should be replaced by hollow wrought iron plate girders: a tender of £28,700 was submitted for dealing with both the bridges. When the line was built, the Dinting Viaduct had cost the SAuL&M £32,000 and that spanning the Etherow, at Mottram, £20,000. The company accepted Fairbairn's tender in November, 1859 and his company, William Fairbairn & Sons, of Manchester, got the work under way immediately. Construction was begun on the Etherow Viaduct first and all was completed by the Spring of 1860. The task was accomplished with no interruption to rail traffic. The new girders were fabricated alongside the track on the approach embankments and run out over the viaducts on bogies, the original timber structures being retained for this purpose. The girders were then lowered into position on the stone piers.

Time, traffic and weather have taken their toll on Fairbairn's ironwork. In 1894 inner lattice girders were added to Dinting Viaduct and extra brick support piers have been added to both structures later on. Seven piers were used at Dinting and were added between 1918 and 1920. Special oak packings were used beneath the bottom flanges of the inner and outer girders.

The name "Woodhead" has, of course, long been used as an appellation for the route as a whole. This is not without significance as the famous, perhaps infamous, tunnel was undoubtedly the keystone around which the entire line was set. An initial plan, of 1836, set out to build the tunnel as a two-track affair. Later economies resulted in a single-line structure of 3 miles, 22 yards: the longest tunnel then extant on the British Railway system. Prior to the opening of the Severn Tunnel, in 1886, it was overtaken in length only by Standedge Tunnel which was just forty yards longer than Woodhead.

Construction began on July 31st.1838 with the sinking of the first borehole by Vignoles. It got under way properly in September the following year after completion of moorland cart roads and the necessary stables and accommodation for the handling of materials. In 1842 contractors were appointed by the company via the recommendation of Locke. Richard Hattersley was to build the western section and Thomas Nicholson the eastern side. Tenders to the value of £39,000 and £45,000 respectively were let. If our present-day Channel Tunnel is, indeed, the wonder of the last two decades of this century, then, to the Victorians, the three miles of bore at Woodhead must have been seen in similar light by them.

Excavating through solid rock with the aid of copious quantities of gunpowder is an extremely hazardous business. In addition, the discovery of hidden springs giving forth vast quantities of water greatly impeded progress. Construction lasted over six years and at one time employed around 1,500 men although the average at any one time was nearer to around 400. Pay for the labourers was between four and six shillings a day (20-30p) and such sums were regarded as being very generous at that time.

Conditions under which the men laboured were little short of diabolical. Paradoxically, it was not under after the tunnel was completed that controversy arose over the conditions that the men had endured during the six year period of construction. The contoversy was wrought by Edwin Chadwick, a Barrister and Secretary to the Poor Law Commissioners, Robert Rawlinson, Engineer to the Bridgewater Trust and John Roberton, a Surgeon and President of the Manchester Statistical Society (a phrase which, incidentally, originally dealt with political science connected with state affairs). Their report (papers) was a damning condemnation of the conditions suffered by railway navvies. Appropriately enough, Roberton's paper dealt with injuries and fatal accidents suffered by the men: 32 were killed, 104 fractures were occasioned and 140 other severe cases of injury were recorded. With health and safety legislation unheard of and beer on sale at 6d. a quart, it was little wonder that drunkenness and even alcoholism among the men was common.

Forms of Syphillis, too, were rife, something hardly surprising considering that many of the men employed on the tunnel brought along

Manchester London Road, c.mid-1890s: Thomas Parker had introduced his Class 3 2-4-2 tank engine design in 1889, fulfilling an urgent need for a powerful and reliable workhorse for suburban passenger work. No **583** was built at Gorton in January 1893, one of 12 built by the MS&L, the remaining 27 being turned out by contractors Neilson & Co; The light green livery, bordered with darker green panels and lettered with plain insignia, contrasts sharply with the later GCR colour scheme as does the plain stovepipe chimney which was replaced after 1900 with one of Robinson's handsome fittings. Allocated to Gorton, Heaton Mersey, Altrincham and Trafford Park, the Class 3 tanks (LNER F1) were one the mainstays of the MS&L's suburban work in the Manchester districts in the period depicted. Our No 583 would have been deployed on trains to Glossop and Hadfield, the smart little 6-wheeled coaches in the background doubtless providing a bumpy ride! The four characters posing for the camera would have been fascinated by the photographer and his heavy plate camera and tripod. It is unlikely that any of the men would have possessed a camera, or, sadly, that they ever saw themselves in this photograph. Collection of ***J Suter***

their mistresses and that tales of "wife-swapping" and men selling their wives for the price of a jug of beer were common in Woodhead folklore. The workmen were domiciled in huts which have been described as "filthy dens" and housed as many as fourteen or fifteen men at a time. Consisting of little more than piles of stones with no mortar between and roofs of thatch or clods of earth, conditions inside must have been grim indeed.

To put this situation in context, though, it has to be remembered that social conditions in cities such as Manchester and Sheffield in those days were, also, appalling. The papers read by the three worthies to the Statistical Society were given due publicity in that esteemed northern newspaper, The Manchester Guardian. A staunchly Liberal publication, "The Guardian" ran Editorials under the title: "Moral and Physical Evils in connection with Railway Works." Though most of the allegations in the papers were repudiated by the contractor, Nicholson, the matter reached the ears of the authorities. Peel's government had set up a Sclcct Committee in the House of Commons to look into the plight of Railway Labourers. The Committe was established in April, 1846 and took evidence from thirty one witnesses, including Chadwick, Rawlinson and three others who had been engaged in work on the tunnel. The report recommended, inter alia, that adequate accommodation for navvies be provided and that construction work should not begin until this was in place. The whole affair has been seen as something of a watershed in the gradual improvement of conditions under which such men were to labour.

Notwithstanding these altruistic gestures, however, fate dogged this second tunnel project at Woodhead and, during 1849, Cholera struck down no less than twenty-eight people. Also afflicted were some of the workers on the nearby Manchester Corporation reservoir construction at Woodhead itself. The dead were interred in the churchyard at Tintwistle. The second tunnel became the Up line and was opened for traffic on February 2nd.1852. It was connected to the original tunnel by 25 passageways spaced at intervals of around 200 yards apart.

In the interim, the short section of line to Glossop had been opened: to goods traffic on June 9th.1845 and to passengers on June 30th. This year, 1845, was a truly momentous one for the SAuL&M: for now, works between the eastern side of the Woodhead Tunnel, via Dunford Bridge, and Sheffield were nearing completion. Intermediate stations-at Dunford Bridge, Penistone, Wortley, Deepcar, Oughty Bridge, Wadsley Bridge and Sheffield itself were opened. The first terminus in the city was sited at Bridgehouses and consisted of a single platform which was used for both arrivals and departures. Regarded as only a temporary measure, Bridgehouses became a goods depot when Victoria opened in 1851.

In similar vein, at the Manchester end of the line, the Store Street terminus was a simple affair and consisted of two platforms set astride a series of tracks set around short turntables. The name "Bank Top" was also used for the station before "London Road" was applied, probably in 1846 when the MS&L was came into being.

The Directors of the SA&M travelled over the line from Sheffield as far as Dunford Bridge in June, 1845. With little ceremony, the entire stretch of railway from Manchester to Sheffield, opened for business on July 14th. A ceremonial opening of both the Woodhead Tunnel and the whole line was carried out on Monday, December 22nd. 1845. Drawn by two locomotives, the train left Sheffield at 10.05, reached Dunford Bridge forty-five minutes later, and arrived in Manchester at 12.15. Conditions in the tunnel and the unheated carriages must have bordered on the diabolical. The train and its party sojourned in Manchester for a mere thirty-five minutes before setting off again for Sheffield.

The Manchester Guardian reported that the two locomotives used were Nos. 17 and 19, both products of Messrs.Sharp, Roberts and Co. A stop was made en route for the party to inspect the Dinting Viaduct. The passage of the Woodhead Tunnel was completed in thirteen minutes and Sheffield was reached at twenty minutes past four. In a style typical of that attending the opening of so many railways, the guests partook of a dinner, held at Cutler's Hall. The number attending was recorded as 230 "gentlemen," along with "a number of ladies." The proceedings were enlivened by music played by the Cavalry Band of the West Riding Yeomanry.

After what must have been a lively evening accompanied by toasts and speeches, another train left for Manchester at 9.30 p.m. Given the form of the two previous trips, some six and three-quarter hours must have been spent by some members of the opening party in rail travel on one single day. Given two, possibly three, trips through the Woodhead Tunnel and between eighty-odd and a hundred and twenty three or so miles of what can only be termed "basic" rail travel in a single day, we can only suppose that the guests were glad to be home! Manchester Clerks, upon request, were treated to a dinner at a price fixed at a maximum of 5/- (25p) per head! It is good to note that the men engaged on the Woodhead Tunnel construction were not forgotten and were given a bonus of £1 each. Those employed by contractor Hattersley were treated to portions of roast beef-the entire carcase was suspended on a makeshift spit made from a length of rail. Knowing well the profound unsuitability of many parts of a beef carcase for roasting, it is to be hoped the men had good sets of teeth!

As the line settled down to earning its living it soon became apparent that a single bore tunnel at Woodhead was inadequate. As a consequence in 1847 a contract for £147,680 was let to George.C.Pauling for the construction of a second tunnel. In the meantime, the Manchester, Sheffield and Lincolnshire Railway had come into being (Incorporated July 27th.1846). Rails through the new bore were in situ by the end of August, 1851. The company profited from the earlier experiences in constructing the first tunnel and more attention was paid to the welfare of the workers. A school was set up at Woodhead and a visiting minister from Penistone was engaged to look after the spiritual welfare of the men and their families. The Reverend gentleman was even given free travel to Woodhead: truly, the company must have been concerned!

So was formed one of the nation's first great trunk railways. The Manchester, Sheffield and Lincolnshire Railway came into being in 1846 upon the absorption of the original SAuL&M Company, The Sheffield and Linclnshire Junction Railway, The Great Grimsby and Sheffield Railway and The Grimsby Docks Company. Just over half a century later, in August 1897, the MS&L, formed originally by a group of men who wished to build just over forty miles of line between two great northern cities, was engaged upon a great thrust south: the London Extension of what was about to become the Great Central Railway. In the latter half of the twentieth century, the route of the original SAuL&M company would become the first wholly electrified railway in the country. Yet amazingly, long before the centenary of the formation of the Great Central, almost all of these two original great Victorian rail projects would have been wiped from the face of the earth.

Thus was born, and died, the SAuL&M and its successors.

E.M.Johnson,
Burnage, July 1995

Manchester Piccadilly September/October 1960, 10.55 a.m: In complete and utter contrast to the MS&L views EM2 Co-Co No.**27001** *Ariadne* awaits departure from platform 1 with the 5-coach 11.10a.m. express to Sheffield Victoria. Since the late 1950s London Road has seen a renaissance and is now Manchester Piccadilly. The MS&l/GCR platforms were later identified as A,B & C with those on the LNWR side beginning at No.1 All that has long been swept away and now the former GCR platforms start at No.1, fluorescent tubes hang where once primitive glass globes shone. Since the 27th.of September electric services have been running on the ex-LNWR side as far as Crewe. Over on platform 4 a 25 kV Bo-Bo has brought in the 8.33 a.m. express from Birmingham, due here at 10.38. A stream of passengers trail in exodus from blue and white-painted carriages. Alongside our Sheffield train a 3-car Class 506 EMU set awaits departure with the 11.15 a.m. local for Hadfield. So we see Piccadilly as it had become, London Road as it was. Platform 1 still looks like this today; sadly, it is no longer possible to travel east of Hadfield.

London Midland Region (B.R.)

Manchester London Road, early 1890s: No.**400**, one of Thomas Parker's elegant-looking 4-4-0s of Class 6DB seen in original condition standing on the MS&L's goods yard outside of the main station and above Sheffield Street prior to working an Up Express. Doubtless inspired by Charles Sacré, this design comprised three engines-all built at Gorton in 1888. Notice the superb condition of the locomotive: polished steel cranks, axleboxes and front guard irons, brasswork gleaming and livery of green and chocolate cleaned to perfection. The tender carries an early form of alarm bell, linked by a cord to the train. Notice the terraced houses in the background built almost to the edge of the railway-here was Duncan Street, Exmouth Street, Chesterfield Street and Malaga Street-all long since swept into oblivion. No.440 was renumbered 511 in November 1893. As 511B, she survived the Grouping and was withdrawn in November, 1923. *Author's collection*

Manchester London Road, c.1913: The pride of the Great Central's locomotive fleet in this period was the splendid-looking "Sir Sam Fay" 4-6-0 express passenger design. Resplendent in Brunswick green, with crimson splasher panel and frames, polished wheel tyres and brasswork, No.**423** must have looked a sight to behold as departure from Platform "A" with the 3.40 p.m. train to London Marylebone was awaited. *Author's collection*

Manchester London Road, "A" Platform, 1947: Almost on the same spot as No.423, thirty years separate the design of the two 4-6-0s. One of Edward Thompson's LNER B1s, a class introduced in 1942, No.**1188** patiently awaits departure in the direction of Sheffield. Appearing in Apple Green, lined black and white-such colour must have appeared more than welcome after years of drab wartime black, and worse. 1188 is almost new in this picture, having been turned out from Vulcan Foundry in July, 1947. She was allocated to Gorton Shed for the first three months of her life and was scrapped in 1965.

Gordon Coltas

Manchester London Road, September 9th.1953: Though we are concerned essentially with main line trains from the former Great Central side of the station, other services belonging to the former owning company are worthy of a glimpse also. Here ex-GC C14 4-4-2 Tank No.**67448** pulls away with the 12.15 p.m. to Hayfield. Overhead, a newly erected catenary support heralds the onset of the electrification programme whilst workmen carry out refurbishment of the glazing in the 75 foot width of one of the train shed roofs.

B.K.B.Green

Manchester London Road, GCR side, pre-WWI: A splendid picture epitomising what would have been a typical local working over the western end of the Woodhead Line in the period before the First War. Parker Class 3 2-4-2 Tank No.**583** waits just outside the station, near a point roughly where the GCR's signalbox stood, with a train of 6-wheeled stock. The engine and carriages are typical of formations used on the London Road to Glossop and Hadfield services up until the early 1930s when the push-pull sets took over. The water tanks in the background were a familiar feature outside London Road for many years. Dominating the skyline is what was then a goods warehouse and a shed for wool, paper and rags standing at the back of the LNWR's low-level goods yard which was situated at the junction of Travis Street and Sheffield Street. *P.F. Cooke*

London Road, ex GCR side, c.1900-1909: Charles Sacré's tenure as Locomotive Superintendent on the MS&LR lasted from 1859 to 1886. The little chap seen here, No.**416**, was one of his Class 18T Saddle Tank locomotives; 41 of these were built at Gorton in the years 1871 to 1881. The engine is on the goods lines which extended from here (a position similar to that of No.583) into the Ducie Street goods yard. Shunting duties only were the employ of the "Humpies" as they were nicknamed, as braking power was limited to just a handbrake. Typical ex-MS&L gas-lit, 6-wheeled local stock is seen in the form of a 1st/3rd Composite No.145 standing alongside. All the 18T class were rebuilt by Robinson with a shortened saddletank and enclosed cabs from 1903 to 1914. No.416 was altered in December 1909 (though some superficial modifications had been carried out in 1900). Withdrawal took place in May 1922. *P.F. Cooke*

Manchester London Road, c.1957: A view from one of the ex-LNWR signalboxes-London Road No.2-of the track layout in and out of the station. The signalbox in the middle foreground dated from the early 1900s when a programme of widening of the LNWR's lines, enabled by an Act of 1898, was instituted between here and Ardwick. The box controlled the Great Central's tracks, on the right-hand side of the station, via pneumatically-operated signals and points. Containing a frame of 82 levers, the box-designated plain "London Road"- was a feature here until the commissioning of the new London Road power box parallel with the electrification to Crewe in September, 1960. The Great Central's Grain and Goods warehouses can be seen in the far right-hand corner. *Dr. J.W.F. Scrimgeour/Courtesy Signalling Record Society.*

Manchester London Road, June 3rd.1954: Last days of steam on the Woodhead line. A3 Pacific No.**60049** *Galtee More* pulls out of the station with an express for Marylebone. Just ten days of steam operation are left before all services on the line are turned over to electric traction; a unique first for a British main line railway and ending the reign of the steam locomotive that lasted almost 109 years. To the right of the engine are the various LMR and ER Goods Lines feeding the ex-London Road and Ducie Street depots of the LNWR and GCR. *B.K.B.Green*

Manchester London Road, May 13th.1958: One of a series of official views taken from the ex-LNWR signalboxes on the station's approaches and immediately prior to the commencement of work on the Manchester-Crewe electrification programme. Here we look from London Road No.2 box towards the terminus and see at once the vastness of the approaches and the sheer complexity of the track layout at this joint station. The Great Central's side of operations began over to the right with the Ducie Street warehouse rising above all and the Grain Warehouse just in front of it. These warehouses, and that of the LNWR, were fed by a series of Goods lines on the extreme right of the view. Next to the goods warehouses is one of four train shed roofs; that on the right covered the G.C.company's three platforms-the erstwhile A,B and C. The ex-Great Central signalbox just peeps behind London Road No.2 box in the mid-foreground. This side of the station has been all-electric for almost four years now; soon work will begin on the ex-LNW side. Catching centre stage, a "Jubilee" runs in with an express; whilst a "Jinty" simmers alongside one of the turntable roads. Over on the MSJ&A platform a 1500v Dc EMU has come to a stand. Notice, on the extreme left, the footbridge connecting London Road to Mayfield Station-a far-flung outpost of the main line station on the other side of Fairfield Street. *British Railways*

Manchester London Road, April 25th.1957: A look inside the former GCR pneumatically-operated power box. The frame housed 82 "levers" or, put more correctly, "slides" which controlled the various points and signals; above these can be seen the indicator lights which showed their positions-either normal or reversed. Presiding over all is the layout diagram with red lights to indicate the occupation of the track circuits. Block instruments are of the type with illuminated positions for the respective indications-similar instruments could be seen in boxes further along the line. Beneath the slides are the small panels with details of each one; these were made from "Traffoylite"-a plastic laminate which revealed a black surface when details were engraved on the white top layer. Extra equipment has been added in the rexine-covered boxes on the left-hand side; this is probably in association with the conversion to colour light signalling that took place after the electrification. A traditional touch is provided by the sight of the polished hand lamp on top of the box-notice the duster and tin of metal polish! Sillhouetted at the window are the signalmen who have, obligingly, popped outside out of the photographer's way. The clock shows 12.55 p.m. In one minute the All Stations via Hyde to Macclesfield Central will leave from platform 1; the slides pulled out from the far end of the frame may well have just set the road. *Dr.J.W.F.Scrimgeour courtesy of the Signalling Record Society*

Ducie Street Goods Yard, early 1900s: The entrance to Ducie Street Goods Yard as it was around the turn of the century. In this picture, packed with all the hustle and bustle of day-to-day working life, we can see the tremendous reliance placed by the railway companies on horse-drawn transport. Reflecting on this golden age, though the steam locomotive, that most revered of man's machines, reigned supreme as a prime mover of traffic for any distance, it was down to the humble horse, one of man's oldest and most loyal animal friends, to move both goods and passengers from the train to their final destination. Prior to the First War there were over 27,000 horses owned by the railway companies and in use for shunting and haulage purposes as depicted here. What an amazing variety of activity can be seen in this little cameo: fine-looking beasts clip-clop resoundingly over the cobbles heading empty carts lettered "Great Central Railway" and returning from their trips in and around the town. Leather apparel appears to be de rigeur for the Draymen who lead their white charges back into the yard, no doubt, to collect yet another load. The character on the right of the picture, with his cap, weather-beaten features and rugged white beard looks as if he would be equally at home on the storm-tossed deck of a sailing ship. Nearer to the camera a man struggles to wheel his animal round. His cart is laden with full sacks-at least 36 appear to be loaded on the waggon-giving a load of around 5 or 6 tons as a minimum. Bringing up the rear are carts loaded with crates, one is lettered "MR", another, to the rear, carries several barrels. Furtively watching the camera, a small group of men stand by the GCR's "London Warehouse", a seven-storey building that would have housed a vast range of merchandise. Notice the steam waggon (N 333) standing by the entrance-a portent of things to come. Over the warehouse entrance a board proclaims the message: "Great Central Railway. Goods Enquiry Office Opposite." Behind this office was situated the LNWR's warehouse-the two companies were ever locked in competition at London Road. Two gas lamps atop stately-looking pillars mark the entrance to the yard off Ducie Street itself, an area alive with the movement of goods traffic at this time. The Rochdale Canal's Dale Street basin and wharf were situated behind Ducie Street, a reminder that older forms of carriage were here first. Out of sight, the Manchester & Ashton-under-Lyne Canal terminated to the right of the GCR's warehouse, behind Junction Street. Pre-dating this building, a coal, lime and iron wharf once stood on this site and handled traffic off the Ashton canal. Interestingly, this area is shown as once housing a wharf and stores for the North Staffordshire Railway. The London Warehouse still stands today, a listed building for all to see alongside what is now the entrance to an NCP car park. You can still walk over the cobbles, where once the draymen and their horses, sometimes loved, sometimes cursed, strode out purposefully in the course of their daily toil. There were still horses and carts at London Road in the early 1950s. Alas, they and the railway which they once served so well, have vanished into history. Ducie Street Goods Yard was taken out of use on 29th October 1967.

Author's collection

Manchester London Road, Ducie Street Goods Warehouse, Summer 1921: The raison d'etre of railways was the haulage of freight between major cities. That inescapable fact is not always reflected in books on railways which, for a variety of reasons, tend to show and concentrate on, the more glamorous passenger-based operations and their motive power. Goods facilities at Manchester London Road were impressive with both the GC and the LNWR having their own facilities. The Sheffield company owned a large warehouse building which fronted onto Ducie Street (and still exists today). Between Store Street and the passenger station was the GC's grain warehouse which forms a backdrop to this view of J.G.Robinson's Class 1A 4-6-0 No.**443**. These were a mixed traffic version, with 5'-4" coupled wheels, of the better-known "Sir Sam Fay" design referred to elsewhere. Notice the tender is fitted with an oil tank; oil firing was fitted to three members of the 1A class in 1921 to cope with a national coal strike. The engine has backed onto a train of vans prior to express haulage over the Pennines towards Sheffield. Notice the chimneys of the terraced houses in the background. Atrocious living conditions existed in the centre of Manchester right up until modern times.

Author's collection

EASTERN REGION TRAIN CONTROL-MANCHESTER LONDON ROAD

Throughout this book I have tried to give various snapshots of signals and signalling arrangements as they pertained over the diverse terrain between Manchester and Sheffield. Behind what is broadly termed "signalling", though, lies another strata of operation entirely unseen- not only by passengers, by enthusiasts, but by train crews and, indeed, signalmen themselves. That strata is known as "Control."

Eastern Region Control Offices, March 14th.1951: This view shows controller Alan Wilkinson at control panel section No.3. This covered the line from Mottram No.2 signalbox to just beyond Deepcar station (the branch from Dinting to Glossop can be clearly seen on the far left-hand side of the panel board). Each passenger or freight train in this section would be identified by placing a small tag in the appropriate position on the control board. At the time this picture was taken up to some 14 tags can be seen in place. Spare tags awaiting placement in the appropriate holes can be seen on the holding panel at the back of the desk top. Behind the controller can be seen the switch panel which enabled him to make contact with each signalbox in the section. To the right of this panel can just be seen section No.4 control panel which covered the section of line from Deepcar through to Eckington & Renishaw. This was the furthest outreach of Manchester Control; beyond this, cover was provided by Nottingham Control.

B.K.B.Green

Eastern Region Control Offices, March 14th.1951: This picture shows Controller J.Millward who is seated at what was Engine Power control panel section No.1. This panel covered the distribution of every locomotive working in the Manchester Control district. Each ticket placed on the board would represent a locomotive and what it was doing at that particular moment. Locomotives on Gorton shed which were not allocated to a train would also be shown on this panel. The adjacent panel to this one was section No.2 which covered the line from Manchester London Road as far as Mottram Yard.

B.K.B.Green

Leaving Manchester London Road, March 7th.1957: One of a series of cab views from Co-Co electric engine No.**27003**, later *Diana*, at the head of the 10.30 am Manchester to Leicester train. This picture gives an unrivalled view of the approach tracks in and out of the station before the onset of the modernisation of the late 1950s. The train has pulled away from platform 1 and is heading out into "the sticks" between the terminus and Ardwick. Once through the double slip, the express will draw round to parallel the ER and LMR goods lines that cut in from the left hand side of the picture. Notice the signal gantry in the background with the distinctive GC pattern semaphores over to the left and the squatter LNW-pattern arms on the right. Slender finials top the Great Central posts, flat-caps those of the LNWR. Permanent way gangs are busy in the distance, the lack of any yellow or orange vests is noticeable. *B.K.B.Green*

Manchester London Road, February 26th.1953: B1 No.**61036** *Ralph Assheton* accelerates the five coaches and two vans forming the 12.30 to Leicester Central away from the station towards Ardwick along the Up Eastern Region line. The first two coaches are comprised of a displaced brake third/third articulated pair from the former "Coronation" pre-War streamlined train. Though full electrification between Manchester London Road and Sheffield Victoria is only around fifteen months away, there is little sign of any activity regarding this. The overhead signalbox on the left was designated "London Road No.1" and carried a massive concrete umbrella to protect it from wartime bomb damage. Behind the Express a C13 4-4-2 Tank waits for the road with a following Local. *B.K.B.Green*

Manchester London Road, May 12th.1954: History in the making as the second test EMU working from Glossop into Manchester enters the station. Public services began the following month; a welcome relief for commuters from the ancient steam-hauled stock that had plied the Glossop/Hadfield route previously. The train comprises two MCCW/BRCW 3-car units each made up of a Motor Brake Open Second Class, a Trailer Open Composite and a Driving Trailer Second Class. DTS No.**E59607** heads the formation. The total train weight of the sets was 104 tons,9cwt; power being provided by four GEC 185 h.p. traction motors. Second Class seats numbered 150, First Class 24. Becoming Class 506 in the BR scheme, these 1500v Dc EMUs last saw service on Friday, December 7th.1984. After that, the rump of the once-splendid GC line was converted to 25kv Ac and standardisation ruled the day. *B.K.B.Green*

Interior of 1500v Dc EMU: One of the first pictures of the new electric stock for the electrified Local services: Manchester London Road-Glossop/Hadfield. To quote the press release: "The interiors are lined with Birch and Sycamore veneered plywood in natural white wood finish. The ceilings and spandrels being painted cream. The large windows are framed in dark Teak. The seats are covered in moquette, blue in the smoking sections and russet elsewhere." *British Railways*

Ardwick, Approach to Carriage Sheds, September 2nd.1954: Right up until the departure of the Class 506 EMUs in 1984 the former Great Central side of Manchester London Road retained its "two company" status. LMR coaching stock was housed at Longsight, ER stock at Ardwick. Here a pristine-looking Class C13 4-4-2 Tank No.**67437** enters the sidings alongside the carriage shed with a rake of main line stock, probably a Marylebone-Manchester train. A Gresley Buffet Car-E41651E-heads the ensemble. Notice the staggered nature of Ardwick's two platforms. *B.K.B.Green*

Between Ardwick and Ashburys, March 7th.1957: The section of line between Ardwick and Hyde Junction had been quadrupled and re-signalled in 1905/06, part of a dynamic programme of works instituted by the Great Central around that time. Here, the 10.30 to Leicester is about to pass a returning EMU to Manchester (notice the "Hadfield" destination!). The train is running along the Up Main line; off to the left is the Up Goods line with the EMU just about to pass the point of commencement of the Down Goods line. Beyond the main line, away to the left, is part of the extensive goods yard once owned by the GCR at Ardwick. This was bounded by the Midland Railway's Ancoats Branch, the same company's Ancoats goods depot and the Ancoats Junction Line-a solid-packed mass of railway lines over a quarter of a mile wide! The large building alongside the Down line belonged to the Vaughan Crane Company and was built on the site of Galloway's Boiler Works. The building survives in use today as C&W Production Engineering, part of the Vaughan Industrial Estate. Galloway's Works and an adjacent iron foundry were served by a series of sidings radiating from nearby Bennett's Sidings which in turn fed into a Goods and Mineral yard referred to as the "Kobo" sidings, belonging to the LNWR at the back of Devonshire Street.
B.K.B.Green

Ashburys (for Belle Vue), April 14th.1951: Ex-Great Central Class C13 Tank No.**67419** pulls into Ashburys with the 12.22 (Saturdays Only) Manchester London Road to New Mills. No less than six coaches on such a service seems like so much largesse these days; but this was an era when many people still worked on Saturday mornings and few had a car. The lower quadrant signals atop the the magnificent lattice post gantry protected Ashburys West Junction from where the former Midland lines mentioned previously diverted. Dating from the installation of low-pressure pneumatic signalling between London Road and Hyde Junction over the period 1904-1909, the pneumatic system was the brainchild of A.F.Bound, the GCR's brilliant young signal engineer. The signalling operating system was renewed between Ardwick and Hyde Junction, as an electro-pneumatic scheme, between January 1929 and the end of 1930. Enthusiasts would no doubt have relished a ride in the former Great Central 50'-0" Clerestory coach immediately behind the engine's bunker.
J.D.Darby

ASHBURYS (FOR BELLE VUE)

The Ashbury company, more correctly The Ashbury Railway Carriage and Iron Company Ltd., of carriage and wagon building fame, gave their name to the station adjoining their premises. These were bounded by Pottery Lane, Ashton Lane (later Ashton Old Road), the GCR main line and Gorton Lane in the Ardwick district of East Manchester. John Ashbury had been given land of an area of just over one acre for part of his carriage works by the MS&L in exchange for a strip of land on the north side of the railway some 175 yards long west of Pottery Lane. The agreement is dated December 31st.1864 and is shown clearly on an official map as "for widening company's railway." Though emphasis is invariably placed on the MS&L/GCR presence in this vicinity, the Midland Railway had considerable territory in this part of Manchester. The company had extensive coal, goods and cattle handing facilities, complete with wagon repairing shops, on the north side of the MS&L/GCR yard at Ardwick and bounded by Gorton Lane and Ashton Lane (both thoroughfares later adopting the "Road" suffix.) Midland territory began west of Ashburys Station at Midland Goods Junction (renamed "Ashburys West Junction." in 1889) This junction served the Ancoats Goods Warehouse (opened in 1870) via the Ancoats Junction line which bisected the Midland and MS&L's Ardwick yards) and the line to Midland Junction where the L&Y's line from Ardwick to Philips Park (opened 1848) was met.

To the east of Ashburys station the Midland's line from Romiley Junction (The Manchester and Stockport Line-Sheffield & Midland Joint) met the MS&L. This is Ashburys East Junction, one time just plain "Ashburys Junction" before the existence of Ashburys West. An Act of Parliament dated 1888 was required to enable Midland trains coming off the Joint Line at Ashburys East Junction and passing through Ashburys Station to cross from MS&L tracks to the Ancoats Junction line.

Ashburys Station, 1960s: Green-liveried Co-Co No **27003** *Diana* (through whose windows we have obtained our splendid cab views) comes through on the Up Main with a five-coach express. In the background, "Crab" 2-6-0 No **42876** blows off impatiently on the Up Goods with a through freight. To the right can be glimpsed part of Ardwick East goods yard, once an important freight complex in this part of Manchester. The train is about to cross bridge No 6 which carries the railway over Pottery Lane. This structure dated from May 1936 when a road improvement scheme was carried out and at the time of writing, history was repeating itself as the A635 road was widened yet again. Sadly, this resulted in the demolition of the remaining buildings on Ashburys Station which dated from the early days of the Manchester to Sheffield line, the station opening in 1855. *Diana* had been christened in January, 1961. She was withdrawn in October, 1968. ***Graham Whitehead***

Ashburys East Junction, June 9th.1953: The overhead catenary supports span the tracks in readiness for the tracery of wire which will be installed over the next few months. Electric traction will see the end of sights like this-V2 No.**60890** has cleared Ashburys station and is seen crossing Ashburys East Junction with an Up Express. The line cutting in from the left is the former Sheffield (GC)& Midland Joint line from Romiley. This route represented the Midland Railway's second attempt to thrust their way into Manchester by means of a joint arrangement with the MS&L. The line travelled via Bredbury, Reddish and Belle Vue to reach Manchester London Road, an accord which lasted until 1876 when the Midland were given three years notice to quit the station. The buildings on the far right belonged to Messrs.Crossley Brothers of motor vehicle fame; the company had private siding accommodation in this vicinity. On the main line, Ashburys sidings and the Gorton Works complex are just ahead; the entrance to Belle Vue shed, belonging to the former Midland Railway, is just down the Branch. *B.K.B.Green*

Between Ashburys East Junction and Gorton, February 1st.1953: C14 4-4-2 Tank No.**67447** clears Ashburys East Junction makes heavy weather up the 1-in-173 towards Gorton with 5 coaches forming the 1.30 Manchester London Road to Macclesfield (Central). Notice, again, the encroaching steelwork for the catenary and the lattice post signals in the background protecting the junction. The impeccably tidy permanent way and freedom from overgrowth are worthy of mention. *B.K.B.Green*

Ashburys, January 31st.1954: The old order changeth.....an unusual shot showing the wiring train in the process of putting the final touches to the overhead catenary system. The train is propelled by 04/1 2-8-0 No.**63611** with an LNER standard 20T Brake Van. In front of this is a classic ensemble for coaching stock buffs in the shape of six ex-G.N. 6-wheel clerestory coaches. All are heavily modified for specialist use; the clerestories have been cut down, the roofs flattened and bars appear over most of the windows. Overhead, the men give the appearance of circus trapeze artists with ladders precariously balanced between roofs and wire supports. The character above the last coach of the train looks particularly vulnerable! *B.K.B.Green*

Approaching Priory Junction, March 7th 1957: The "Juice Engine" at the head of the 10.30 to Leicester is now well into her stride as Priory Junction looms ahead. Sited 2 miles, 14 chains from London Road, this was the point where the Great Central's famous locomotive works and running shed was accessed from the main line; the train is just about to negotiate the pointwork. There appears to be plenty of activity on shed: the line of wagons on the left appear to be loaded with ash. Ahead, on the right, is Priory Junction box and, just in front, the crossovers from Fast to Slow lines. ***B.K.B.Green***

Priory Junction, July 7th.1951: J11/3 No.**64316** passes the junction and associated signalbox with an Up 5-coach local train. The splendid array of semaphores off to the right relate to the goods lines and read as follows: i) (l to r) Down Goods Home to Main (Inner Distant for Ashburys East beneath), ii) Home for Down Goods (towards Ashburys East), iii) Down Goods to No.1 loop, iv) Down goods to No.2 loop v) (just out of the picture) Down Goods to Coal Hopper. The small semaphore below the gantry controlled exit from the shed to the Down Goods line. The connection between the junction and Gorton shed yard was severed on November 21st.1967. *B.K.B.Green*

GORTON-A THUMBNAIL SKETCH

Though the popular name for the shed and works of the former Great Central Railway has always been "Gorton", it was actually in Openshaw, then a semi-rural village to the south-east of the centre of Manchester, that the Manchester, Sheffield & Lincolnshire Railway established a locomotive works and running shed in 1846. Hitherto, the Sheffield company had established workshops near Hyde in what were little more than wooden huts. We have already mentioned Richard Peacock, a Yorkshireman by birth, who became the company's "engine driver No.1." Peacock was charged by the railway with finding an alternative site for a works and had set his sights nearer to Manchester, alighting on what appeared to be a prime site. The land on which the works complex was built was acquired by the MS&L from one George Cornwall Legh and extended as far east as the canal aqueduct. Separate acquisitions of land, from John Eaton and Aaron Lees, were required on which to build the later Gorton Station. Legh's name lives on today in Cornwall Street which separated the works from the old Gorton Station. On a point of minor interest the MS&L were required to pay Legh total annual Chief Rents of £3701-10-3d, a huge sum of money in those days.

The Openshaw district was served by a Turnpike Road, then named Ashton Lane (later Ashton Old Road-A635) and the Stockport Branch of the Ashton under Lyne canal; the newly-opened line to Sheffield passed nearby and a small population, then engaged in the trade of hat manufacture, were close by. Moreover, the adjacent land was level and the Openshaw township was then independent of big brother Manchester. This gave Peacock an added incentive in the form of lower local rates. In a paper read to the Institution of Mechanical Engineers in January, 1851 he concluded "*......with the advantage of being situated near enough to a First-class mechanical town to secure any that may be had therefrom, it is sufficiently far out of it to be clear of the heavy local taxes with which such establishments in all large towns are burdened.*"

"Gorton Tank" was joined in 1854 by the locomotive building works ("Gorton Foundry") of Beyer, Peacock & Co. Sited on the south side of the main line and founded jointly by Charles Beyer and Richard Peacock himself, Beyer, Peacock became a world-famous institution and a household name all over the globe wherever locomotives were wanted from the United Kingdom. Some 66% of Beyer, Peacock's production was exported at one time. Ashburys Carriage and Wagon company had been established in 1837 and neighbouring Sir Joseph Whitworth (later Armstrong-Whitworth) a heavy engineering company who also had locomotive building interests-opended a works to the west of the Gorton empire in 1880. Whitworth obtained his land from the MS&L under agreements dated January 22nd.and August 17th.1877 respectively.

This conglomeration of engineering enterprise was augmented by the factory of Crossley Brothers on Pottery Lane, to the north of the railway, who produced gas and oil engines and became involved in car and bus production as well. (An official MS&L map gives Crossleys the suffix of "Otto Gas Company Ltd.") The company was founded in 1866 by Francis William and William John Crossley and became remarkably successful. Francis William Crossley moved to Ancoats, then a slum area, to work amongst deprived people-a benefactor indeed. The company moved from Openshaw in 1947 to a works alongside the LNWR Manchester-Stockport line at Errwood Park, Heaton Chapel. The old Openshaw building, now carrying the famous Rolls-Royce emblem, is currently being substantially rebuilt as part of the A6010 road improvement scheme. The name of the Crossley company lives on in Crossley Road in the Burnage-Heaton Chapel districts.

Dotted around Gorton Works in the early years of this century were also various chemical works, a rubber works, a cotton mill, several sundry engineering works, a horse shoe manufactory, a boiler works and two or three iron works. Small wonder, then, at a remark I heard some years ago from a lady whose husband had been a Gorton employee and who had grown up in the area: "if you tried to cross Chapman Street at six o'clock in the morning, you ran a fair chance of being knocked over by a bicycle!"

Gorton Works and shed had never been a big place, hemmed in as it was by the Great Central main line to the south, the Ashton under

Gorton Coaling Stage, n.d: *Sir Sam Fay*, now re-numbered as LNER **5423**, alongside the Gorton coaling stage. Prior to the introduction of the mechanical coaling plant, in 1932, wagons of loco coal were propelled up a short incline to the back of the stage before the fuel was shovelled into steel, wheeled tubs. These were then pushed forward towards the front of the stage and the coal was tipped into the respective bunkers or tenders. All an incredibly laborious, dirty and time-consuming task which must have been a thoroughly unpleasant job for all concerned! An identical process survived at neighbouring Heaton Mersey until the shed closed in 1968. *Gordon Coltas*

Lyne Canal to the east, Ashburys Sidings, Armstrong Whitworths and Openshaw Goods to the west and Whitworth Street to the north. The entire nucleus of Great Central locomotive building and repair work, coupled with the company's carriage and wagon building activities had at one time been contained in an area of around some 40 acres. As with any large railway establishment, Gorton Works had progressivley grown bigger since its inception. New carriage shops were commenced in 1880; an enlarged erecting shop was added, possibly in 1882 and built on land to the west of Wellington Street - a thoroughfare which had acted previously as the dividing point between the stabling and construction sides of the Gorton complex in pre-"Birdcage" days. In 1895 a new administrative and office block was opened facing onto Cornwall Street. New machine shops and stores were added in 1888/89 and in 1900 a new locomotive paint shop was opened on the west side of the loco running shed behind Whitworth Street. The original arrangement for stabling of locomotives was in a large roundhouse with seventeen radiating roads. A more conventional arrangement, with parallel roads, was instituted in two stages-in 1875, giving ten roads and 1891 which added a further ten. A map in my possession, from the archive of the late V.R.Webster, records stabling for 120 locomotives c.1880. Upon completion of the later sheds, the roundhouse (or "Rotundo") became absorbed into the works complex and was used as a Smithy.

Elementary education was not made compulsory in this country until 1876, so something of a forward-thinking attitude had been taken by the MS&L at Gorton in 1855 when a school for the children of the company's work force was opened. Extended in 1889, and with 1,182 pupils on the roll-a mixture of infants, boys and girls-the school was built on land next to the works on land bounded by Cornwall Street, Ogden Street and the Manchester & Ashton-under-Lyne Canal. In typical Victorian manner infants and girls were taught in a separate building to boys. The school shared a plot of land with the MS&L's canal works; the boys' playground rubbing shoulders with a stables and urinals!

Records of locomotive allocations just prior to the Grouping show 178 engines based at Gorton shed. The later running sheds were sited on the north side of the complex, hemmed in by Wellington Street and Whitworth Street. Flanking the running shed were carriage and wagon building and repair facilities. By the end of the century, the MS&L had become the Great Central Railway and had opened a new and costly main line to London. Expansion of the company's activities resulted in the removal, in 1910 of carriage building and repair work to a large new factory at Dukinfield-about ¾ mile east of Guide Bridge station on the south side of the main line and facing Dewsnap Sidings.

In common with many locomotive depots Gorton underwent a programme of modernisation in the early 1930s. The double-sided coaling stage was replaced by a mechanical coaling tower; its concrete, tower-like form-brought into use in 1932-was no doubt responsible for the slightly irreverant nickname of "The Cenotaph." At the same time wet ash pits, to aid locomotive disposal, were brought into use along with adjacent new loco coal sidings. The ash pits were amongst the largest on the LNER and were sorely needed, some 250 tons of locomotive ash per week were reportedly removed at Gorton in its heyday. A sundry, though famous, feature of the Gorton shed and works site was the footbridge known as "The Birdcage" that led from Railway Street, on the south side of the main line, across the complex to Wellington Street (later re-named Widnes Street) between the running shed and the works. Installed in 1879 and built by the Manchester firm of De Bergue & Co. this bridge must have been used by thousands of Gorton men over the years; it outlived the closure of the shed and works before being removed on January 8th.1967 by the Longsight breakdown gang using a steam crane.

Gorton had established a sound reputation for locomotive engineering and this was complemented by the fine products of Beyer, Peacock & Company whose plant was sited nearby. By the early 1960s the railways of this country were undergoing a major upheaval with closure and rationalisation occurring with ever-accelerating pace. Gorton shed itself had already absorbed part of the locomotive allocation of the nearby ex-Midland depot of Belle Vue when this closed in 1956. Already taken over by the London Midland Region two years later, Gorton shed closed for good on June 12th.1965.

The works was to be similarly afflicted: one of the highlights of the twilight years was the cosmetic restoration, in 1961, of D11 Class 4-4-0 "Butler-Henderson" one of the second batch of "Directors" built at Gorton for the Great Central Railway between 1919 and 1922. The last engine to undergo a heavy repair at Gorton was Stanier 8F No.48520. After this, casual repair work was done with BR Standard 9F 2-10-0s - the locomotives concerned being Nos.92419, 92161 & 92215. 92161 was the very last engine to leave Gorton after a "casual repair". Looking through the Drawing Office Register the blue-penned writing comes abruptly to an end half way down the page. The last entry, dated January 18th.1963, lists drawing No.18632 for a driving shaft, part of a lubrication oil pump for a Crossley HSTVEE Diesel engine. The draughtsman, one V.W.Kingsley, used a scale of 6"/ft. for his historic drawing. None of the foregoing appeared in the press at the time, although The Manchester Evening News carried a feature on the closure of the works that year. In typically lugubrious journalese it was headed: "When life suddenly shunts you into a siding." Heavy with emotion about loyal railway families, the situation was, of course, ripe for a good piece of journalism about a local community. Particular play was made about the story of the projected batch of 54 Bo-Bo "Hymek" Diesels which were planned for production at Beyer, Peacock. The Gorton men, understandably, regarding the work as having been "stolen" from them. In the end, Peacocks only built 36 engines and then they, too, were destined for closure.

Gorton Shed Yard, c.1923: An early evening scene on Gorton shed in early pre-Grouping days dominated by a splendid view of No.**426c** *City of Chester* (the suffix "c" indicated Central Division of the LNER). Notice the general debris littering the scene-ash and clinker from fire-dropping interspersed with broken firebars. Above No.426's cab can be seen the Boiler Shop chimney, one of dozens of such slender brick edifices whose outpourings of smoke and soot characterized much of industrial Lancashire. The three locomotive tenders make for interesting comment on Great Central and early LNER engine liveries. On the left-hand side is the tender of No.470, a B7 (9Q) 4-6-0 with 5'-8" coupled wheels built at Gorton in 1922; this is finished in black with red and white lining. *City of Chester* appears in LNER Apple Green lined black and white, to become the standard for the company's passenger engines. Notice the retention of the GC's distinctive oval brass numberplate on the cab side. On the right is D9 (11D),No.1024, one of J.G.Robinson's first 4-4-0s, built in 1902 by Sharp, Stewart & Co. 1024 appears, also lined black and white, but set off on a backcloth of the Great Central's superb darker shade of passenger green. *P.F.Cooke*

Gorton Foundry, early 1950s: As the Great Central main line ran eastwards, it formed a boundary between the Gorton Works and Shed complex owned and operated by the railways themselves and the works of Messrs.Beyer, Peacock & Co., a private company who enjoyed close links, not only with the Great Central-for whom they built a considerable number of engines-but also other companies both at home and abroad. Heading towards Manchester is B1 No.**61195** with a Down express; notice the pair of former LNER streamlined coaches behind the Brake Third. In Beyer, Peacocok's yard one of their many overseas products stands, probably awaiting removal to Manchester Docks. The photographer is standing on the bridge over Preston Street. The trackwork in the foreground gave the company access to the main line. *Author's collection*

After the site had been cleared, the new Manchester wholesale fruit and vegetable market which had previously existed on a very cramped site by Oldham Road near to the city centre, was built on the land mapped out by Richard Peacock back in the first half of the nineteenth century. Of Gorton Tank and Works-where generations of lads, Fathers and Grandfathers toiled in the grit of the ashpits, the sweat of the Smithy and the din of the Erecting Shop, nothing remains.

Gorton Works, 26th September 1961: One of the most poignant tasks in the closing years of Gorton Works was the restoration of the prototype of the D11 (11F) "Director" Class 4-4-0 No.**506** *Butler-Henderson.* Though a splendid job was done in bringing a real Great Central locomotive back to life, several features of the restored engine were not authentic: in particular, the smokebox with its snaphead rivets round the circumference- a feature of new smokeboxes in LNER days and most un-GCR like. This aside, the sight was, indeed, a splendid one and is made here all the more so by the presence of four former Great Central drivers. Left to right are Vinson Gulliver, Bert Wagstaffe, an unknown driver and Arthur Davies. Vinson Gulliver began work in a cement works in Warwickshire. He came to Manchester on February 2nd.1907 to work at Trafford Park loco and retired in 1953. Amazingly, at the time of writing, Vinson is still with us, having attained the incredible age of 107 years; making him the oldest man in Britain and, almost certainly, the oldest surviving railwayman in Europe. *W.A.Brown*

Gorton Works, July 1920: A feature covering Gorton, its Works and men, would not be complete without some reference to that most celebrated engine No.**1165** *Valour*. Turned out from Gorton in July, 1920 this engine was the third of J.G.Robinson's Class 9P (LNER B3) four cylinder 4-6-0s which eventually numbered just six locomotives. *Valour* was dedicated as the Great Central's war memorial engine and a special nameplate, cast in the shape of a shield, was fixed to the engine on building. It read: "In memory of G.C.R. employees who gave their lives for their country 1914-1918." As can be seen, the nameplate covered almost the whole of the depth of the splasher panel; in consequence there was no room for the customary positioning of the builder's plate and this had to be fixed on the outside cylinder cover. No.1165 was held in great affection at Gorton and for many years was specially cleaned, decorated with a commemorative wreath on the nameplates, sometimes on the smokebox too, and worked to Sheffield Victoria on the 8.20 am from Manchester London Road to Marylebone to take part in the annual Armistice Day commemoration service for the 1,304 men of the Great Central who had been killed on active service in the First War. *Valour* was withdrawn in December, 1947 as LNER No.1496. One of her nameplates was placed in St.Barnabas's church in Openshaw and was, sadly, stolen. The other can still be seen in the National Railway Museum at York. A fine testament to the sacrifice of so many splendid young men. *National Railway Museum*

Gorton Works, Erecting Shop, n.d: The expressions on thirteen faces are frozen for a brief second in time in this most fascinating view inside the works revealing GC locomotives in various stages of repair. Five men, sober-looking characters, stand behind Great Central Atlantic No.**1088**-one of twelve 4-4-2s built by the North British Loco Co. at their Hyde Park Works, Glasgow in 1905. Two more men pause at the front of the engine, seemingly engaged on some task behind the smokebox. Notice the two youngsters sat in the Atlantic's cab; they seem little more than children, remember the school-leaving age at one time was a mere fourteen years. The photographer is perched on top of an 8A (LNER Q4) 0-8-0 which is bereft of boiler, smokebox and motion and has been lifted off its wheels-seen on the left. Various machines were driven from the long countershaft that can be seen running in plummer blocks beneath the roof girder on the left hand side of the shop. Exposed belts and a multitude of moving parts were considered par for the course in those less safety-conscious days. Fitters' vices over on the right await components-all part of the process of maintenance and repair that was the bread and butter of the men of Gorton.

Public Record Office, London

Gorton Works, n.d: The works in modern times, no Great Central types are to be seen now and the shops will have entered their latter years. Left to right, a 9F 2-10-0, an O1 2-8-0 and O4/8 No.**63706** can be seen undergoing various stages of repair. Notice the various bits of tubing scattered about and the ubiquitous jacks. The white markings on the various engines were always unintelligible to the outsider; in skilled, hands, though, all went back together and emerged fit and sparkling for duty once more. *N.E.Stead*

Gorton Works, 23rd April 1963: As mentioned in the text, the last locomotive to be repaired at Gorton was Stanier 8F 2-8-0 No.**48520**. By a strange touch of irony, 48520 was built not by the LMS, but by the LNER at Doncaster in October 1944 as part of Lot No.167, Works No.1968. The engine was on loan to the LNER from the date of building to November 1946 when it was transferred to LMS stock. Here, posing for the local newspaper report is that celebrated last engine with some of the men who worked on her appearing in the photograph. Twenty-eight faces appear in this view; sadly, for many of these men, this will be almost the last time they will work as craftsmen. And for men like Arthur Richardson, works convenor and Herbert Wainwright, the closure of the Works was the end of their working lives. A great shame, indeed, that a lifetime's commitment had to end like this. Thus, in a scene attended by what was probably a mixture of sadness, resignation, disappointment and, doubtless, anger No.48520 passed out of Gorton Works yard. The 8F went back to Speke Junction shed (8C). It was withdrawn from service in September 1966 and stored at its home shed until January 1967. Gorton's final engine was cut up at Draper's in Hull in February that year. Another page in the chapter of steam locomotive building and of Great Central history had closed. *Reporter Group of Newspapers*

Gorton Works, Main Entrance-May 1963: The Gateman watches and a touch of melancholy is in the air as a group of ten men leave the works for what is possibly the last time. 1,700 men had been employed at Gorton Works in its latter years. The closure of the works had a devastating effect on the local community here, an effect that was to become more and more widespread as rationalisation of railway workshops became increasingly commonplace. In the background the scroll over the window reads "M.S.L.Ry.Co. In between the second and third man on the left-hand side can be seen the War Memorial tablet fixed to the wall which is inscribed: "GORTON WORKS IN MEMORIAM 1939-1945." Some 29 names appear, a sad and poignant reminder of human sacrifice. *Reporter Group of Newspapers*

Gorton Shed Yard, 1963: A view from the "Birdcage"-bridge No.9 looking across to the Carriage shed-a building erected in 1881, to which the inscription on the end tower testifies. Taken for local newspaper publication, the photograph is captioned "Gorton Tank About to Close." Along the siding roads can be seen well over 20 locomotives; most are 2-8-0 variants, though a J11 has been slipped in. Long out of steam, many are daubed with the fateful "X" indicating impending cutting-up. Identifiable as such from this parade of moribund motive power are (l to r) 04/3 No.**63713**, 04/6 No.**63631** (centre) and Austerity 2-8-0 No.**90391**-near rhs, behind the coal heap. Ensconced in the midst of these lifeless ranks can be seen two 9F 2-10-0s, possibly these are the engines on which minor repair work was done in the very last days of the works. *Reporter Group of Newspapers*

Gorton (Old) Station, early 1900s: A Parker Class 2 4-4-0 No.**707** enters the old station at Gorton with a Down passenger working comprising six 6-wheelers and a bogie clerestory carriage. The train has just cleared the original aqueduct carrying the Stockport branch of the Manchester and Ashton-under-Lyne canal over the railway. The aqueduct was built from brick with stone arches and voussoirs. This view makes for a most interesting comparison with its counterpart picture showing the widening of 1905/06. What a fascinating contrast with our later views of A3s, B1s and EM1 and EM2 Electrics! Notice the white sighting boards behind the semaphore signals protecting Gorton Junction; these were done away with when the new aqueduct was built. "Advertise in the Manchester Evening Chronicle-the smartest paper" proclaims the hoarding on the station building. Gorton's cast-iron seats by Andrew Handyside & Co., although associated as standard with the Great Central company, were items of furniture manufactured by the Derby company. The waiting shelter on the Up platform bears a distinct resemblance to that at Hadfield. No.707 had been built by Kitsons in 1892. It acquired a Belpaire boiler in 1909 and was withdrawn, as LNER No.5707 of Class D7, in August 1933. *R.K.Blencowe collection*

Gorton and Openshaw, c.1920: A superb period view showing one of J.G.Robinson's handsome large boilered 2-8-0s (Class 8M) No.**420** pausing with an Up local working. Clearly visible is the "new" station, then at least 15 years old, with four platform faces and lattice footbridge (designated No.11A). No.420 was converted to burn Colloidal fuel (a mixture of oil and pulverised coal) in January 1920. The oil was housed in a tank on top of the tender; clearly outlined in this picture and reaching to the extremes of the loading gauge. Colloidal fuel was part of a series of experiments by Robinson to find an alternative to conventional lump coal for locomotive working; No.420 covered some 38,000 miles with this type of firing before being converted back to a straight coal burner in October 1923. The engine was rebuilt to diagram O4/6 in September, 1941 and withdrawn from LNER stock at that date for service overseas. *National Railway Museum*

WIDENING OF THE LINE AT GORTON 1905/06

Standing on the run-down, unstaffed platforms of Gorton station today and watching the Class 305 EMUs, the 158 DMUs interspersed occasionally with Metro-Cam DMUs en route to Marple, New Mills and Sheffield we gaze upon a railway altered out of all recognition from that at the turn of the century. Such was the volume and density of the traffic at that time that the Great Central, flushed with pride at the opening of the London Extension to Marylebone, and with the dynamic and energetic Sam Fay as General Manager, embarked, inter alia, with an ambitious re-modelling programme between Ardwick and Hyde Junction.

An act for the widening of the main line between Manchester and Hyde Junction had been obtained as far back as 1866 and was repeatedly renewed until, in 1902, it was decided to go ahead with the actual construction. The work was divided into three portions: the first section commenced at Ardwick and terminated 580 yards east of Gorton (old) station. The second part continued as far as Guide Bridge and the third continued to Hyde Junction. Contractors were engaged by the Great Central for the first two portions; the company themselves engineered the third part.

At Ardwick a new loop on the Down side of the line was provided. This commenced about 300 yards west of Ashburys West Junction signalbox and ran for about half a mile before regaining the main line just beyond the Down platform there.

Of particular note was the provision of quadruple track between Priory Junction, Gorton and Guide Bridge itself. From this unique series of photographs, possibly the work of a photographer employed by Messrs.Hemingway & Company of Nottingham, the contractor for this section, we can view a detailed record of the works around Gorton at this time. A separate contractor, W.Pattinson & Sons, built the new Gorton station.

Gorton (Old) Station, 1905: Taken from the south side of the aqueduct that carried the Stockport branch of the Manchester and Ashton-under-Lyne Canal over the railway, we look on the original station at Gorton, the site of which dated from May, 1842. A huge quantity of earth has been removed to make way for the new track formation and a massive retaining wall, a superb piece of Edwardian craftsmanship, provides a backdrop. The wall, 20 feet high, was made from concrete, faced with blue engineering brick. Three workmen on the platform gaze up at the photographer. A frock-coated figure, probably the Gorton Stationmaster, in like manner, stares similarly while keeping a discrete distance from the men. Remember, this was an age when social distinctions were still very marked. Down on the new formation, workmen sit around-rails and sleepers providing impromptu seating for this is lunchtime, or-as contemporary Mancunians might have said: "time for us snap!" Notice the provision of a shunting neck, for Gorton Works sidings, beyond the newly-laid Up line. Beyond the new canal aqueduct can be seen the lattice footbridge that led down to the canal depot here. The signals feature prominently: the Distant arm in the foreground relates to the curve round at Gorton Junction (Q.V.) and would have been controlled by Hyde Road Junction signalbox. *Collection of B.Longbone*

Gorton Old Station, looking east: A view, packed with interest and one which complements the previous picture taken from the aqueduct. The overbridge, complete with water main carries Cornwall Street which leads into Chapman Street and Railway Street; the latter a thoroughfare which paralleled the main line. The widening proper started roughly at this point and tied in with the formation leading from Gorton Works-seen off to the bottom left. In the middle background can be seen the originalGorton station which dated from May, 1842. Through the haze towards the Lees Street overbridge can just be glimpsed the semaphores, and the signalbox controlling Gorton Junction. The Gorton station Down Home signal towers above the Cornwall Street bridge; the Distant is for Priory Junction-set back towards the Manchester direction. This lofty "peg" has co-acting lower arms to aid sighting. Of special interest is the signalbox controlling the layout at Gorton Station-an early timber-framed structure seen on the right-hand side by the overbridge. With its slated roof and centre ball and spike finial, the sight of this building gives us a valuable close-up of one the earlier signalboxes on this line which are totally dissimilar from the later MS&L/Great Central pattern. Similar structures existed at Hazelhead and Thurgoland. Immediately across from the box, almost camouflaged by the new brickwork, can be seen an MS&L-pattern semaphore. Notice the abandoned "Gorton Station" sign lying in front of the new bridge-what might this have fetched at today's Railwayana auctions? The gas lamp by the new bridge abutment may have been to illuminate a walking route to and from Gorton Works. A temporary wooden footbridge down to the old station and the contractor's locomotive immediately adjacent are worthy of study.

Collection of B.Longbone

Gorton Widening, 1905/06: The newly-built canal aqueduct seen from the east side of the new works. This was a complete replacement for the old structure which consisted of two stone arches, one for each line. The lattice-steel footbridge led down to the canal depot and connected with the passageway behind Varna Street school. Little or no interference was made with the canal traffic while the new aqueduct was constructed. A temporary wooden trough for boats to pass along was laid on half of the old canal bed. The new structure was then built in the position occupied by the remainder of the width of the old aqueduct. Part of the brickwork for the new Gorton and Openshaw Station can be seen rising from the "six foot" between the old and new tracks.

Collection of B.Longbone

Lees Street overbridge, looking east c.1905: Commensurate with the widening a new station was built at Gorton. Named "Gorton and Openshaw", it served all four lines and was sited east of Gorton old station between the canal aqueduct and the Lees Street overbridge. In our view the contractors have completed the new platforms, but beyond the overbridge there is still work to do: the trackwork has yet to be completed for what will become the Down Slow line; in the distance the boom of an excavator can be seen dressing the soil at the top of the cutting. Work has yet to begin on replacing the overbridge in the distance; this carries Vine Street-connecting Ashton Old Road to Abbey Hey Lane. Problems were encountered on this section with slippery ground forming the cutting. In consequence a small retaining wall (a "toe" wall visible in the picture) and an open drain were constructed to facilitate soil retention and keep the sides of the 22 ft. cutting intact. The ground beneath the track here consists of wet clay and required deeper excavation than normal. An extra foot of depth, packed with ashes provided the base for the new trackwork. Hand-packed rubble was placed on top of this to a depth of 9". Top ballast and trackwork were then put into place. Care was taken by the company to ensure the new trackwork bedded in thoroughly: a special traffic notice for the Manchester District dated week ending October 12th.1907 stated that *the new lines between Priory Junction and Stockport Junction will be used for goods trains only and that a speed restriction of 35 miles per hour would apply*. The Lees Street overbridge, numbered 12 in the Guide Bridge district register, was sited 2 miles, 60 chains from Manchester London Road and about 215 yards east of the canal aqueduct. It was built with steel longitudinal girders and jack arches. The width between the parapets is quoted at 42 ft. Off to the left the steelwork for the new station entrance rises from the ground, an untidy jumble of scaffolding poles. Six of the seven contractor's men stare at the camera, a seventh engages another in conversation while the moment is recorded for posterity. Notice the lattice steel signal posts and spectacles ready for their arms and pneumatic apparatus-a contemporary "state of the art" system. Just visible through the bridge is Gorton Junction signalbox and the curved trackwork of the Manchester Central Station Railway of 1892 branching away towards Hyde Road Junction. The new station opened for passengers on August 25th.1906.

Collection of B.Longbone

Gorton and Openshaw, May 2nd.1953: An interesting comparison with the 1905 view is provided by the sight of B1 No.61195 enteringthe station with a Down Express. From a similar viewpoint we can view the rather unusual style of brickwork forming the entrance from Lees Street. Notice the splitting Home signals for Gorton Junction have been moved over to the right-hand side of the line from their original position to improve sighting.

H.F.Wheeler
R.S.Carpenter collection

Aqueduct, Manchester & Ashton-under-Lyne Canal-Stockport branch: The presence of the busy main line of the Great Central Railway is betrayed by the myriad of telegraph wires which appear spun, weft-like, above the still waters of the canal meandering through the newly-constructed aqueduct. Our view looks north towards Openshaw itself and Clayton. The building on the immediate right is Varna Street School-a rather foreboding-looking building; the alma mater, no doubt, of many an artisan who worked for the Great Central. Behind the school is High Bank Mill which was in fact an engineering works at the time this photograph was taken. Across the canal the depot buildings stand out, complete with gasometer (or gas holder). In the distance can just be seen the overbridge which carried Ogden Lane over the canal en route to Clayton-a district renowned for its involvement with the chemical industry. Ogden Lane-a thoroughfare teeming with tiny terraced houses which stood up to the late 1970s. Here lived the men from Gorton Works, from Gorton Shed, from the canal depot and from industry all around. A microcosm of Manchester's industrial might at this time: all vanished now-the canal had become derelict by the 1950s and was subsequently drained and filled in. Today, with the surrounding area reclaimed and landscaped over, only the aqueduct is left; the towpath survives intact, beneath, the recessed platework that once held the murky waters of the canal lies choked with weeds and the detritus of the modern world. ***Collection of B.Longbone***

Gorton Station, March 7th.1957: It was the district of Gorton that gave the name to the well-known works and shed complex which we have just left; though this, as stated, was actually sited in Openshaw. Here, again from the cab of *Diana* en route to Sheffield, the four track formation outside Gorton Station is clearly visible, with the sweeping crossovers from Slow to Fast lines prominent in the foreground. Gorton Junction signalbox is tucked almost out of sight at the near (Manchester) end of the Down Fast platform. The overbridge ahead is the aqueduct taking the Stockport branch of the Manchester & Ashton-under-Lyne canal over the railway. On the immediate left can be seen the footbridge to the canal depot referred to elsewhere. Much has changed in the intervening years: the canal was closed c.1963/64 and subsequently filled in. It is at about this point today that the four track formation ends, the old Slow lines being lifted from here eastward towards Fairfield. *B.K.B.Green*

Hyde Road Station, August 21st.1958: A picture taken by the official photographer to record bridge No.8-the underbridge carrying the Chorlton Junction to Fairfield line over the A57-the Manchester to Sheffield Road. To give it its full title-"Hyde Road for Belle Vue"-this was the fourth station on the 6 miles, 30 chains of the Manchester Central Station Railway opened throughout on May 2nd.1892. Hyde Road, with its wooden platforms, differed, as did to some extent Fallowfield, from its counterparts down the line at Wilbraham Road and Levenshulme. This short section of railway, something of a backwater and mentioned only rarely in railway literature, was of major importance to the Woodhead route. Over this bridge passed countless trains from Liverpool and Merseyside-freights, coal and passenger-to emerge onto the main line at Fairfield and bound for Guide Bridge, Dewsnap Sidings and beyond through "the hole under the hill." Notice, too, the catenary-for just down the line is Reddish traction depot which, together with the new Woodhead Tunnel, had become symbols of the new age for this part of the former Great Central main line. The elegant chimneys, attractive cupola, curved lintels and inlaid brickwork all give us something to marvel at in an age when suburban railway stations are becoming increasingly like bus shelters. Though closed to passengers on July 7th. that year, the view gives no hint of impending doom. Marie Celeste-like the deserted platforms appear clean and swept, station signs are in place and gas lamps stand intact and seemingly ready for duty. The fine Great Central-style wooden signalbox at the far end of the left-hand (Up) platform will stand for many years yet before it, too, vanishes-destroyed by fire in November 1988. The site of Hyde Road station had one last moment of glory when, for one week in February 1987, a series of demonstration runs were made from here down the line towards Reddish in a London Docklands LRT vehicle. This was to give various officials and the general public a foretaste of the "Metrolink" system then being planned for Manchester. But back to 1958: a corridor coach, possibly of GER origin, can be seen in the goods yard. The latter was the only point where trams and trains interfaced within the Manchester City boundary. *British Railways*

Hyde Road, August 21st.1958: Though its primary interest is merely to show the underbridge (No.8) spanning the A57 road I felt this picture had such depth of social and local colour that it merited inclusion. The railway's photographer was kept busy here-he took over forty whole plate shots of this bridge, obviously some major construction work was pending. Looking down to road-level, could main roads have ever been as quiet as this? The pictures were taken on a Thursday; any weekday these days would find this road absolutely teeming with traffic-yet then only two vehicles, an Austin A35 (UNF 362) and a touring coach could be seen. Two buses and a cycling policeman have just passed by as well! Look at the fine station entrance by the bus stop: a tall imposing brick structure with stone pinnacles and carved stonework reading "1892 Hyde Road Station. " How many of you Mancunians remember those curious green-painted street lights with their scrolled necks dotted here on the edge of the pavements. The couple, doubtless a Mum and Dad, seen passing under the bridge are holding on to their little boy; almost certainly the family will be bound for Debdale Park, a local attraction just around the corner where the advertisement hoardings proclaim "Fray Bentos Corned Beef", "Haig Whisky", "Guinness" and "Cleveland Discol-the high octane petrol with alcohol-for all cars." Waiting at the bus stop is a young lady who has just crossed the road from Willow Grove. Smartly dressed and complete with earrings, high-heeled shoes and handbag she was obviously off to meet someone. At the end of her journey on either the 57, 77, 109 (to Reddish), 136 or 210 (the Trolleybus that terminated at Hyde, Gee Cross), someone would be looking forward to meeting her. A sweetheart of nearly 40 years past, I wonder who she was? *British Railways*

Reddish in the Making, January 11th.1950: Class 04/8 2-8-0 propels a train of materials on to the site of the embryo traction maintenance depot. Notice the steel frame of the depot rising in the background.
William.J.Skillern

REDDISH CAR SHEDS-A BRIEF DESCRIPTION

Under the initial proposals for the Manchester-Sheffield electrification project it had been intended to accommodate electric traction, along with repair of locomotives, in a portion of the existing steam running shed at Gorton. Practicalities must have sunk in during the war for, on August 22nd.1947, The Railway Gazette announced in an article on the forthcoming project that..."The main electric and repair shops and running sheds will be situated at Levenshulme (sic), six miles from Manchester, and there will be smaller running sheds at Darnall (near Sheffield) and Wath."

Whether the fault of the LNER press release or a simple ignorance of the geography of south-east Manchester, the site chosen for the proposed depot was in fact at Reddish, actually a district of Stockport with virtually the entire boundary sited within that Borough.

The depot was to be sited on a piece of land known as Melland's playing fields. The land straddled the boundary between Manchester and Stockport and housed three small reservoirs. One of these had to be drained to accommodate the new depot. The site was accessed directly from the Fairfield-Chorlton Junction line and was situated between Levenshulme South and Hyde Road stations. Access to and from the depot was controlled by Hyde Road signalbox. Hyde Road box controlled a junction at the apex of an inverted triangle: northwest the line ran round to Gorton Junction, giving direct access to Manchester London Road. North-eastwards, the trackwork continued towards Fairfield; thus access to the new depot was enabled from three different directions.

With the land suitably prepared, the steelwork for the depot structure was well in hand by the end of 1949. Materials for the depot proper were being delivered in January 1950; though it was Summer 1954 before the whole building was completed and ready for operation. The depot was fully equipped for servicing both EMU and main line locomotives alike. The main repair shop, 400' long, was saddled by offices and workshops on one side, with an inspection bay on the other. A 35-ton overhead crane and an under-floor wheel profiling machine were added later on. Separate facilities existed for the repair and servicing of pantographs. No mechanical washing plant was ever installed for EMUs-even the prestigious Midland Pullman Diesel-electric sets, stabled at Reddish from 1960 onwards, were washed by hand.

Conceived as an all-electric servicing and repair depot, Reddish never really reached its full potential in this role owing to the later adoption of 25 Kv Ac as the BR electrification standard. Writing in the programme for Reddish's only Open Day-held on Sunday, September 9th.1973, Mr.D.J.Whincup, the area maintenance engineer there, remarked how the depot's fortunes had changed over the years and that, then, over half the work done involved Diesel traction in one form or another.

But by 1973, the word Rationalisation was eating into British Rail, as indeed it had been doing since the onset of Beeching in the 1960s. The Co-Co (Class EM2) electric locomotives had gone and inside the next decade, the Woodhead line itself would be extinct as well.

Looking at the photographs taken of Reddish depot during and after construction is to gaze on something of a paradox. For, new as the all-electric technology appeared, it was already out of date. Though set as the standard back in the late 1920s, 1500v Dc was not the way forward. Contemporary railway literature looked favourably on the achievements of the French 25 kv Ac system and, within only four or five years of Reddish's birth, such a system was being installed in South Manchester for the Crewe electrification programme which was to become the precursor for the West and later, East coast main lines.

Reddish Electric Depot, May 4th.1954: An historic moment in the Woodhead electrification scheme as Bo-Bo No.**26040** arrives at the depot; the first electric locomotive to do so. The building, still incomplete, looks pristine nevertheless with the usual hallmarks of new construction surrounding it-piles of bricks, whitened windows, contractor's plant and scatterings of debris. All very much part of a new age, which for this railway would be, sadly, short-lived. *B.K.B.Green*

After the closure of the Manchester-Sheffield-Wath line in 1981 the depot remained open to maintain and service the Class 506 EMUs which were used on the Manchester-Glossop-Hadfield services. These were eventaully serviced at Longsight, something which caused a little difficulty as they had to be towed dead under the 25 kv Ac overhead.

Many Electric locomotives of Class 76 were left at Reddish on closure of the Woodhead line and these were eventually sent away for scrapping or were cut up on site. Some of the 76s were really only body shells, having been stripped of essential parts and bogies from time to time in order to keep the rest of the fleet operative.

A number of supervisory and shed staff remained behind at Reddish after the line closed in order to strip the building of essential useful parts and also to act as round the clock security. At this time it was rumoured that there was a possibility of Reddish remaining in use for other functions. Options considered were:

a) The depot would be taken over for Tamping Machine maintenance and other useful storage/maintenance facilities by BR Civil Engineering staff.

b) The depot could be used as a maintenance centre for the projected "Metrolink" system as there was a possibility that this might be extended to take in the Glossop-Hadfield services. There is no doubt that Reddish would have been an ideal candidate for this function as it was fully equipped with inspection pits, overhead crane, Matterson lifting jacks and a fully operating wheel re-profiling machine. Full workshop facilities existed, along with a pantograph overhaul shop, to say nothing of excellent staff facilities and easy road and rail access.

In the end, none of these options was taken up. The British Rail staff finally left Reddish sometime during 1983, but not before an expensive security fence was erected around the entire depot premises. Though a security company was contracted to guard the depot, 24-hour cover was not maintained and it was only a matter of days before the depot was broken into, severely vandalised and what equipment was left inside was stripped out and stolen.

In March, 1987, GMPTE ran a converted Docklands Light Rail vehicle on a demonstration pre-"Metrolink" weekend trial along a short section of the Fallowfield line from a temporary wooden platform near Hyde Road Junction. Passing Reddish Depot on the short run was a somewhat sad experience. A vast hulk of a once-busy building wasting away amid a wilderness of natural overgrowth.

The final irony may occur when the trams roll across the site of the former Chorlton Junction, possibly before the year 2000, en route to Manchester Airport. Looking for fresh fields to conquer and new markets to exploit, who knows whether Metrolink may well push along towards Fallowfield, Levenshulme and Reddish. Perhaps then the planners will discover the system needs extra accommodation for its electric traction....

Reddish Electric Depot, May 28th.1954: This was the east end of the depot; the view is taken from the main entrance which was sited off Greenlea Avenue/ Wayland Road South. The Ryder Brow housing estate, which fringed onto the depot, was the home of many of the men who worked at Reddish. On the left of the picture is the servicing shed. The middle part of the building, with its raised section, was used for major overhauls and later housed an overhead crane and wheel lathe. On the right-hand side were offices for the rolling stock inspector and the shed foreman. *British Railways*

Reddish Electric Depot, May 18th.1954: A view inside the Inspection Bay, looking east. The council houses located on Greenlea Avenue, which overlooked the depot yard, can just be seen. Just visible, through the far doors, are the overhead stanchions and the trackwork curving away down the Fallowfield line. The depot already has two "customers" in the shape of a pair of Bo-Bo electric locomotives. The presence of scaffolding and a pair of ladders suggests construction work still in progress. *British Railways*

Reddish Electric Depot, West End. April 9th.1954: A bright, clear Spring day sees the rear of the new depot rapidly approaching completion. The "overhead" is all in place and will shortly be energised to enable the arrival of the first visitors. The first locomotive to enter the depot was Class EM1 Bo-Bo No.26040 which arrived on May 4th. *British Railways*

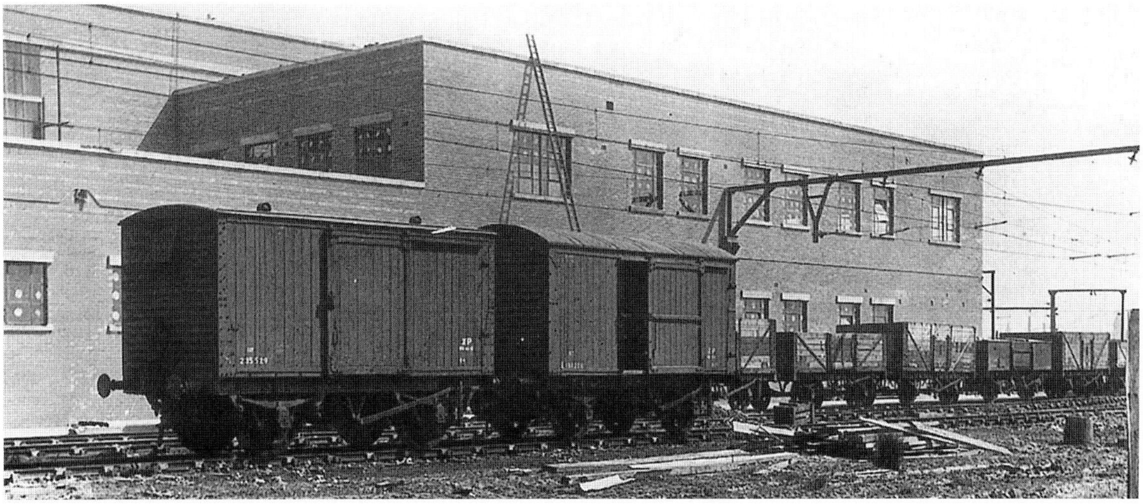

Reddish Electric Depot, May 18th.1954: A view of the west end of the depot. Looking towards the first floor, the first windows belong to the office of the Assistant Depot Engineer, whilst the second set belong to the Area Maintenance Engineer's office. The remainder of the space on the first floor is taken up by the pantograph repair and assembly shop. *British Railways*

Reddish Electric Depot. 6th May 1959. A book covering the MSW electrification and its progenitors would not be complete without a picture of *Tommy*, the pioneer LNER 1500v Dc main line electric locomotive. As LNER No.**6701** the locomotive was assembled at Doncaster with electrical equipment supplied by the (then) Metropolitan Vickers Company. 6701 was completed in August, 1940 and underwent trials on the MSJ&A line in September of that year. The locomotive was stored at Doncaster for much of the duaration of the war before being shipped to Holland in 1947 where it remained in traffic until 1952. Affectionately known as *Tommy* by Dutch railwaymen, after the nickname for British soldiers, the name was officially applied in a ceremony at Liverpool Street station on June 30th.1952. As a member of Class EM1 (later Class 76) *Tommy* was taken out of service on February 9th.1968, only to be restored to traffic in the summer of 1969. Returned to store in February 1970, *Tommy* was withdrawn the following month and was cut up at Crewe in October 1972. Given the historic importance of the locomotive and its fascinating post-war history, it is surprising that "*Tommy*" was not preserved.

B.K.B.Green

Geldermalsen, Holland, June 20th.1948: Britain's railways had just been nationalised and completion of the Woodhead electrification was still a distant dream when the pioneer Bo-Bo (now re-numbered as LNER **6000**) was caught on film at Geldermalsen-between Utrecht and Einhoven. The clerestory coach coupled behind the modern locomotive looks almost anachronistic. Notice the leather-jacketed Dutch engineman standing beside the front buffer.

K.J.Cooper
Industrial Railway Society

Reddish Electric Depot, October 14th.1955: Maintenance at Reddish has got into its full stride, it is now over twelve months since the Woodhead lined became fully operational. Bo-Bo No.**26004** receives attention to one of its pantographs inside the main repair shop. At the far end of the building one of the flat-topped coaches from the overhead wiring train can be seen. To the right of the shop, drums of cable of varying sizes are housed inside a wired security cage. *British Railways*

Reddish Depot, approach from Levenshulme, 1960: Class 04/7 2-8-0 No.**63734** barks its way up the 1-in-100/108 towards Hyde Road with a train of coal empties en route back, no doubt, to the Yorkshire pits. The bridge in the background carries Longford Road over the railway. Alongside the Up line can be seen part of a trailing crossover and headshunt. This marked the limits of the depot and the termination of the "overhead" is clearly visible. Under the original plans for the Woodhead scheme, drawn up in the late 1930s, it had been the intention to electrify the whole of the Fairfield Loop line along with the ex-CLC sections into Manchester Central and round to Trafford Park. Indeed, drawings exist showing all the intended supports for the overhead catenary. Work was also begun on the station structures, in the form of cutting back of platform canopies to provide the necessary clearances. Unfortunately this point proved to be the limit for electrification; had the original plan come to full fruition then, maybe, the whole of South Manchester's suburban railway system may have taken on a different complexion. *Tom Lewis*

Levenshulme South, September 1961: Right up to closure of Manchester Central in 1969 Harwich and Hull to Liverpool services ran over the "Fallowfield Line." Change-over from Electric to Steam traction took place at Guide Bridge with trains leaving the GCR main line at Fairfield Junction. Throughout the 1950s and '60s A5 Tanks, B1s, Stanier 2-6-4 tanks and "Crab" 2-6-0s put in an appearance on these trains. Viewed from the signalbox, No.**42846** at the head of the 4.35 p.m. from Hull has just passed under bridge No.16-the wrought iron lattice footbridge which led from the alleyway by the UCP Tripe Works across to Jackson's clay pit and brickworks in neighbouring Reddish. The Restaurant Buffet (RB) express was due in Manchester at 7.54 (where reversal took place) and in Liverpool (Central) at 8.53. *Author*

Levenshulme Station, April 4th 1951: A view from the Down platform looking west as J11 No.**64406** slogs through with a train of wagon empties, probably bound for Dewsnap sidings. Local services from Guide Bridge to Manchester Central still had some seven years to run, finishing on July 5th 1958 after which the line survived for another 30 years - becoming a walkway and cycleway under the auspices of Sustrans in 2002. The MS&L must have had high hopes for local traffic. Entering from road-level here and at Fallowfield and Alexandra Park ("Wilbraham Road" from 1923) Victorian feet trod on parquet flooring while daylight flooded in via stained glass windows. Glazed and covered staircases led down (up at Hyde Road) to the platforms. Notice here that the sides and front of the platform canopies have been cut back to provide clearance for the electric overhead line. The Fallowfield line into Manchester Central had been earmarked for electrification under the original MSW scheme, but post-War cost-cutting saw the catenary truncated at Reddish Depot. Still, we now have Metrolink down the line at the erstwhile Chorlton Junction! *Neville Fields/Manchester Locomotive Society*

Chorlton Junction, c.1928: A great trunk route such as the Woodhead line, in similar fashion to a river, cannot function without its tributaries. One such was the Chorlton Junction to Fairfield line-known officially as The Manchester Central Station Railway. This drew traffic, from the Cheshire Lines system and especially Liverpool, and fed it towards the East Coast via Woodhead. Taking the "branch" up towards Wilbraham Road and making a powerful sight in the process, is LNER-built B7 4-6-0 (the former Great Central mixed-traffic 9Q design) No.**5483** with what is probably a cross-country express. In the foreground the territory changes from that of the CLC with the ex-Mildand line carrying on south towards Derby. *G.H.Platt*

Fallowfield Station, c.1945: Fallowfield, the second station on the line out from Manchester, had its own goods yard and at one time boasted a banking engine for assisting heavy freights up the 1-in-100/1-in-80 gradient towards Levenshulme and Hyde Road. This fine Summer shot sees ex-Great Central 4-6-0 of Class B9 (8G) No.**6107** clearing the goods yard en route eastwards towards Levenshulme with a train consisting largely of coal empties. Notice the goods yard full of wagons and the water tank to provide sustenance for the banker. *William Lees*

Wilbraham Road, April 1938: In this splendidly atmospheric scene former Great Central 4-6-0 Class B9 (8G) No.**6114** clatters through the station with a train of coal empties en route eastwards and back to the Yorkshire pits. Despite having their looks slightly marred by rebuilding with a higher-pitched boiler, the class retained much of the Robinson pedigree throughout their 40-odd year lives. 6114 (GCR No.1114) was the last of ten engines built in 1906 by Beyer, Peacock & Co. As 1478 this specimen was amongst the last to be withdrawn, on the eve of Nationalisation, in December 1947. *William Lees*

Fairfield (old) Station, c.1899/1900: Pollitt Class 11 No.**698** pulls hard up the 1-in-100 bank past the site of the old Fairfield Station with a Manchester to Sheffield express. The photograph is taken from the cover of the magazine "Locomotives and Railways" for the month of February 1901. The carriages consist of five six-wheelers, plus a bogie coach and a van of some kind at the rear. No.698 had been built as one of a batch of six engines at Gorton in 1895 under the auspices of Harry Pollitt. These fine-looking 4-4-0s were distinctive inasmuch as they carried the first Belpaire boilers to be fitted to an MS&L passenger engine. A station had existed at Fairfield from the line's inception in 1841, though the original building was little more than a shed. A permanent structure was constructed in 1846 when the line was doubled. Accommodation consisted of a booking office, three sets of waiting rooms and a porters room situated on the Up platform; a single building, designated ladies waiting room, existed on the Down side. Prominent in our photograph is the large Stationmaster's house here at Fairfield which stands out loftily above the train. MS&L line plans show clearly the site of the old station with the buildings, footbridge and signalbox demolished. Fairfield new station, some 370 yards east of the old station, was opened on May 2nd.1892 when the last section of the Manchester Central Station Railway (Chorlton Junction to Fairfield) opened from Fallowfield to Fairfield Junction on the main line. The characters seen walking along the track (following what looks like a well-worn walking route) towards the camera could well be the Stationmaster, complete with frock coat, and, perhaps, a porter. No accommodation for the stationmaster is shown at Fairfield new station on the original plans so, doubtless, the house was retained for this purpose. When the line was widened, in 1904/05, the building seen here would have been demolished as all the works were done on the north side of the line. Just visible in the background are the chimneys of houses on East Bank, a terrace of properties built in 1886 on what was then Station Road. Today, Station Road has become Manshaw Road, doubtless because the road falls neatly on the boundary of Manchester and Audenshaw, now part of Tameside M.B.C. Fairfield's old station lives on in the name of a fine Victorian public house at the top of Manshaw Road and in the terrace of shops named "Station View" across Ashton Old Road.

Author's collection

Fairfield (for Droylsden), April 16th.1954: Class C14 4-4-2 Tank barks away from Fairfield with a stopping train from Manchester London Road to Glossop. Fairfield was at one time a prestigious residential area; J.G.Robinson, the esteemed GCR Chief Mechanical Engineer lived here and would have been a regular commuter down to Gorton. The station seen here was opened in 1892 when the Manchester Central Station Railway (the "Fallowfield Line") was completed from here to Chorlton Junction. The platform layout was altered when the line was widened. At Fairfield the Fallowfield line met the Great Central main line from London Road; the former cuts in just behind the photographer. The C14 is is on the Up Fast line, the Slow lines run between the platform faces on the right-hand side of the picture. *B.K.B.Green*

Fairfield Junction. Summer, 1957. A closer look at Fairfield Junction signalbox. The box is to a typical Great Central design: simple fretted bargeboards with finials between wood planked gable with a four-paned window in the centre and main windows set in a series of three vertical oblong panels. The junction box, housing 44 levers, dated from the inauguration of the low-pressure pneumatic signalling from Ardwick to Newton mentioned earlier. The view looks towards Guide Bridge; the Fallowfield line is on the right. The signals reflect the junction layout: (left to right) Up Fast to Up Slow Home, Up Fast Home, Up Branch to Up Slow Home and Up Branch to Up Fast Home. The lower-quadrant arms on the left are sited on the original lattice steel posts; the upper-quadrants are of a standard B.R. tubular post variety. *B.K.B. Green*

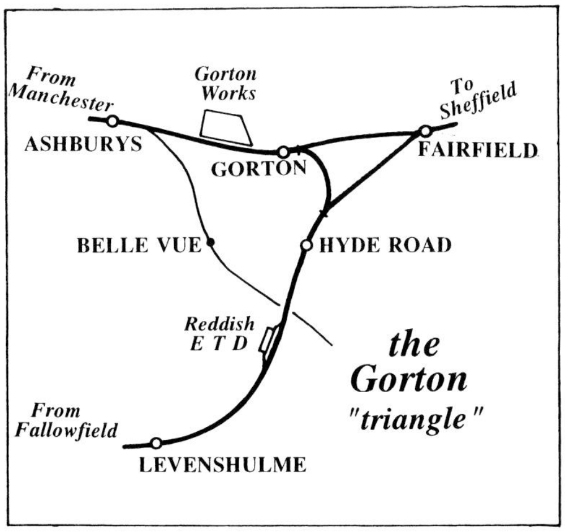

Fairfield Junction, September 12th 1953: B1 4-6-0 No **61312** crosses the junction and heads towards London road along the Down Fast line with the 10.00 Marylebone to Manchester Express. Notice the semaphore in the background (just alongside the fourth coach) is at the "on" position. This will have occurred automatically as the train occupied the track circuit in advance of the signal. ***B.K.B.Green***

Fairfield, April 16th.1954: B1 4-6-0 No.**61159** clears the junction and works steadily along the 1-in-133 eastwards towards Guide Bridge with a 9-coach Express. In the background, a solitary colour light signal has now replaced the splendid-looking GC pattern semaphore bracket viewed earlier. Two items of railway technology at the lineside are worth talking about: supported on concrete posts alongside the Down Fast line is the low pressure air main to operate the electro-pneumatic point and signalling system that had been installed along this section of line by the Great Central. Containing compressed air at 15 p.s.i., the system was fed from a pumping station near Guide Bridge East box. This contained three vertical boilers and two Class A Duplex Ingersoll-Sergeant double-acting air compressors. Of much more recent vintage is the 33kV power cable and pilot cabling for the impending electrification scheme. This is sited just beneath the line of telegraph poles and linked the various feeder stations with the Penistone Control Centre. *B.K.B.Green*

Between Fairfield and Stockport Junction, February 9th.1952: A splendid view of 04/3 2-8-0 No.**63870** as it waits for the road outside Stockport Junction, just west of Guide Bridge. The train, a through freight, is standing on the Up Slow line. Audenshaw Road crosses the line on the skew in the background. James Street overlooks the railway at the top of the cutting. *B.K.B.Green*

Stockport Junction, August 12th.1956: One of the key points on the route-a view looking towards Manchester from the end of platform 3. This picture shows the junction in its entirety with not a complete train in sight! The signalbox seen here dated from the widening of the line between Ardwick and Guide Bridge to four tracks in 1906. The new lines, laid to the north of the existing ones, were brought into use from Gorton to here: Down line on November 11th. that year and Up line three days later. Prior to widening, the layout here was quite different. The old Stockport Junction box was positioned on the north (right-hand side) of the line nearer to the station and Guide Lane overbridge. A double slip connection enabled trains from tracks on the north side of Guide Bridge station to be crossed over to the Stockport line. The actual junction with the OA&GB line was named "Audenshaw Junction East". A separate box-"Audenshaw Junction West" was positioned further down the line, on the south side, and controlled the spur that ran north to connect at Canal Junction.
To return to our picture. The former Great Central main line continues ahead towards Fairfield and Manchester; Audenshaw Road, bridge No.21, spans the four-track layout-the Up and Down Main is to the left, the Slow lines are over on the right-hand side. The OA&GB line towards Crowthorne and Ashton Moss junctions veers off to the right; an A5 tank engine waits its turn to move forward to take a cross-country express from either Hull or Harwich via Fairfield Junction down the Fallowfield line into Manchester Central. Loaded wagons fill Cock Lane sidings-the site of the LNWR's goods yard here. The four track layout with its attendant complexity of switches and crossings to and from three separate routes reflected the intensity of the traffic prevalent here at the time. All incredibly expensive to maintain and eventually rationalised out of all recognition. *Dr.J.W.F..Scrimgeour/courtesy of the Signalling Record Society*

GUIDE BRIDGE-A JIGSAW OF SOME COMPLEXITY

The origins of the rather curious name "Guide Bridge" seem to be somewhat obscure. What is more certain is that the area, really part of the neighbouring Lancashire town of Ashton-under-Lyne, owes much of its development to the coming of two, possibly three, different modes of transport.

What is essentially a rather small district grew up initially as the result of the cotton industry. "King Cotton" had spawned much of the industrial heartland of North-West England in the eighteenth and nineteenth centuries. In and around Guide Bridge he brought his mills alongside ready-made transport in the form of the Manchester and Ashton-under-Lyne Canal and The Peak Forest Canal; thus enabling the movement of raw materials and finished products a feasible and reliable proposition.

Looking at an Ordnance Survey map of the area for 1922 one might be forgiven for thinking that, perhaps, some part of south-west London had become transposed by mistake onto this small corner of north-west England-such is the plethora and complexity of running lines, junctions and sidings packed into a relatively small space. Here, collieries, brick works, cotton mills, a rubber works, gas works and a sewage works rub shoulders with one another and are scattered variously around in what looks at first glance like some sort of random fashion.

A more considered study, however, shows some logic. Logic applied by the railway system which first arrived here in November, 1841.

Guide Bridge's first station carried the name "Ashton and Hooley Hill" and was merely a staging post en route to Godley; this being part of the Sheffield, Ashton-under-Lyne and Manchester Railway's grand scheme of things to reach Sheffield. And that much we have already seen.

"Ashton and Hooley Hill" was renamed "Guide Bridge" in 1845, the year that through services to Sheffield began. Parallel with the opening of the Woodhead Route the 2¼ mile line from Guide Bridge to Stalybridge was inaugurated, opening (as a single line) on December 23rd.1845. Further connections to the district came about in 1845 when the Manchester and Birmingham Railway obtained an Act for the construction of a line from Heaton Norris, where Stockport's first station was sited, to Guide Bridge. The Heaton Norris and Guide Bridge line connected with the MS&L main line at Stockport Junction, just west of the station and opened for traffic in 1849.

An important alliance-the Oldham, Ashton and Guide Bridge Junction Railway, a joint affair owned by the MS&L and the LNWR, had come into being in August, 1857. The railway was spawned as the result of deputations from Oldham and Ashton to connect the two towns with the routes of the L&Y and LNWR in the two towns. Nineteenth century railway politics are everlastingly tedious:briefly, the MS&L had urged the LNWR to join the alliance-but this was to the dislike of the L&Y who withdrew their support for the scheme. The LNWR filled the vacuum and tied the knot with the MS&L. The OA&GB line was leased jointly to the LNWR and the MS&L from June 30th.1862.

The OA&GB had their own station at Oldham Clegg Street and trains continued originally as far as Glodwick Road station which was owned by the LNWR. The line entered the Lancashire mill town from the south on an embankment; there being two intermediate stations on this northerly section: at Park Bridge and at Ashton Oldham Road. A station had also existed at Ashton Moss, an area outside Ashton town centre. Interchange sidings at Ashton Moss for L&Y and GCR freight traffic were part of a development in the district which had been sanctioned by the Great Central Act of August 1909. Included in this scheme was the curve from Ashton Moss South Junction round to join the L&Y main line (Ashton Branch) at Ashton Moss North. The curve, owned solely by the GCR, was commissioned on December 18th.1911. Along with the sidings, the whole project cost £11,329.

Departing north from Guide Bridge, the OA&GB company were forced to use the L&Y's Manchester-Stalybridge (Ashton Branch) route for a short distance before heading north again towards Oldham. Movements fore and aft the L&Y line were controlled by a signalbox called "OA&GB Junction" (Q.V.) Services on the Stockport-Guide Bridge-Oldham Clegg Street line finished on May 4th.1959; Park Bridge and Ashton Oldham Road stations closed at the same time. The station at Ashton Moss had been short-lived and closed as far back as March, 1862.

Coming south from Oldham trains left the station at Ashton, Oldham Road and headed towards OA&GB Junction. After passing Ashton Moss South Junction and travelling towards Guide Bridge, Crowthorne Junction was encountered: here was the LNWR's connecting line known as the Guide Bridge Junction line which ran down to join the Ashton Branch Junction Line (at Ashton Moss Junction) connecting Denton Junction with Droylsden and opening for traffic on February 14th.1876. The plethora of variations on the name "Ashton" round these parts is confusing to the outsider to say the very least!

One of the OA&GB's earliest surviving timetables-published in April, 1863 shows nine trains daily from Oldham's Glodwick Road to Stockport with ten in the reverse direction. The earliest was 7.45 a.m., the last 9.0 p.m. Journey times were in the region of 45-47 minutes. Trains had to reverse at "Guidebridge" (sic) in those days; the connecting line from Crowthorne (Guide Bridge Junction line) had yet to be constructed. No less than four classes of travel are shown: 1,2&3 and that shown in the timetable as "Parl". This was an abbreviation for "Parliamentary", the statutory services the railways were required to run under Gladstone's Railway Regulation Act of 1844. The act stipulated that at least one third class train per day had to be operated over all lines. These were required to be run at not less than 12 mph (including stops) and had to call at all stations. Fares were regulated not to exceed one penny (1d) per mile and the companies were expected to provide carriages which offered protection from the weather.

Guide Bridge (old) Station, c.1900/1904: The earlier station buildings and entrance off Guide Lane as they were prior to demolition and enlargement of the station in 1905/06. Guide Bridge had been enlarged and improved in the early 1870s-the work being finished in 1874. Although this enlarged station had four tracks, there were only two platform faces, a situation which lasted until 1905 and resulted in the buildings seen here being demolished; the latter-day platforms 3 and 4 covered this site. Accommodation in these buildings consisted of (from west to east) left luggage office, stationmaster's office, general waiting room, 2nd. & 3rd. class ladies' waiting room, 1st.class ladies' waiting room, booking office, a second general waiting room, a Midland Railway booking office, porters' room and a gents' lavatory. The Midland Railway presence was reinforced by an office for their agent on the east side of the Up platform. Prior to this date part of the platform area was covered by an overall roof which extended across the tracks to the Up side. Records show this as having been removed in 1899 to allow for the construction of an extension canopy (an "umbrella" in GCR terminology) to cover the whole length of the platform. Notice the earlier signal gantry which was to be replaced by the well-photographed lattice-post version of modern times. Just peeping beyond the gantry is the lattice footbridge spanning the eastern approaches to the station which made its arrival c.1900.

Reporter Group of Newspapers

Guide Bridge, Stockport Junction. no date: B1 Class 4-6-0 No.**61129** crosses the junction on the Up Fast line and enters the station with what, by the looks of things, is a heavy east-bound express. The dwarf pneumatically-operated semaphores were designed to be housed in what was a restricted space with minimal clearance. The group on the left read (L to R): i) Down Fast to Cock Lane Sidings. ii) Down Fast to Fairfield). iii) Down Fast to Down Slow. iv) Down Fast to Oldham line. Notice the arrows indicating the 15 mph speed restriction over both the Stockport and Oldham lines at Stockport Junction.
W.A.Brown

A First Class return from Oldham to Stockport and back cost just 1/11d; Second Class was 1/5d and "Parl" just 11d! Interestingly, the timetable shows connecting services to London ("Euston Square") from Stockport. Trains took a fraction under five hours and fares (return as above) were 33/9, 24/6 and 16/0. Not exactly "Apex" levels considering the wages of 132 years ago!

Continuing to Guide Bridge: beyond Crowthorne Junction, the OA&GB line split yet again at Canal Junction. An 18 chain spur ran south-east to Stockport Junction where the MS&L main line and the previously-mentioned line to Stockport was met. Thus, direct travel from Stockport to Oldham was possible without the need to call at Guide Bridge. From Canal Junction another line ran off south-westwards in the Manchester direction to join the GC main line at Audenshaw Junction. By using this line from Audenshaw Junction to Canal Junction it had been possible for MS&L trains from Manchester to Oldham to by-pass Guide Bridge altogether. The company's trains could reach Oldham in 20 minutes over this route with one stop at Ardwick. Services began on August 26th.1861; passenger traffic ceased in 1863 only to resume again in 1867. Back in 1910 the timetable showed just two trains each day in the Up direction taking this route (at 11.10 am and 11.00 pm). Oddly enough, no corresponding Down service appears to be shown. This line did not survive into modern times and services ceased in June, 1930; though the cutting was later filled in, one "old timer" recalls that Canal Junction box was still open in 1940. Some track had been lifted during the war; but remaining sections, heavily rusted, were still in situ in the summer of 1944. The northerly connection between Stockport Junction and Crowthorne Junction was closed on May 16th.1983. Audenshaw Junction, minus the branch connection to Canal Junction, survived as a set of crossovers from Fast to Slow lines east-bound and Slow to Fast west-bound; the switches were controlled by Stockport Junction box.

Guide Bridge station was enlarged in 1874 and again in 1905/06 when the through lines were quadrupled and four platform faces provided.

Passing through Stockport Junction the GC main line line ran due east beneath Guide Lane where a competing tramway service ran. East of the station, and 354 yards from Stockport Junction, was sited Ashton Junction where the Ashton and Stalybridge line (of 1845) ran in a north-easterly direction to parallel the Manchester and Ashton canal. Here was an extensive siding complex known as Brookside Sidings. Both sidings, railway and canal were fronted by a large complex of cotton mills bounded by Guide Lane, Stockport Road and Grosvenor Street.

Yet another connection was put into the Guide Bridge jigsaw of complexity when a connection running to the north from the east of the station was opened. Known as the Guide Bridge East Curve, sanctioned with parliamentary powers obtained by the GCR in 1900, the connection ran from Guide Bridge East Junction, 585 yards from Ashton Junction, and joined the Ashton & Stalybridge line at Guide Bridge North Junction just by the previously-mentioned Brooksdie Sidings. It was opened for traffic on January 23rd.1905.

Just past Ashton Junction the Woodhead line crossed yet another railway; this time belonging to the LNWR. This was the Denton and Dukinfield line (or "Stalybridge Junction Line") which had left the Heaton Norris and Guide Bridge line at Denton Junction. The "Hooley Hill" name had been used for a station on this line to serve the district of the same name; the station was re-named "Audenshaw" in June 1924. This railway was a relative latecomer to the Guide Bridge district not opening (for passengers) until November 1st.1882 and enabling trains from Stockport to Stalybridge to by-pass Guide Bridge. The line originally extended to Dukinfield, but opened through to Stalybridge for goods traffic on August 1st.1893 and for passengers six days later.

Stockport Junction, signalbox interior-August 12th.1956: A first-rate view of the frame and its attendant technology. Prominent are the operating handles of the 36-slide frame for the points and signals. These aspects of the signalbox hardware dated from 1906 when the original 15 p.s.i. pneumatic operating system was installed. Re-signalling from Ardwick to Hyde Junction cost the Great Central just over £45,000-a huge amount of money in pre-inflationary days before WWI. The chosen system was of American origin and was brought to the LSWR by Sam Fay then company Superintendent of the Line. Traffic density at Stockport Junction in 1900 was prima facie evidence for the provision of power signalling. No less than 265 Down and 252 Up trains passed this junction, via a double track system, in one 24 hour period in a traffic census taken in the July of that year.
In the intervening years, early 1930s, the original low-pressure operating system was replaced by am electro-pneumatic one. Further modernisation has resulted in electric light block indicators: red for "train on line" and green for "line clear", along with a BR standard fully illuminated track circuit diagram. The operating slides had slots cut into them in which rollers ran to drive the mechanical interlocking. A slight resistance would be felt by the signalman when pulling a slide from its slot. Once the train was clear of the appropriate track circuit the slide would return to its original position automatically. Normal and reverse indicator lights can be seen above the respective slides.
In later years, following a serious derailment at Audenshaw Junction in May, 1970, covers were placed over the slides to prevent the "false feeding" by signalmen of the signal slides and thereby short circuiting the electrical delay mechanism. Bi-directional working was in force on all four lines through Guide Bridge station-from Stockport Junction to Ashton Junction-and permissive working of freight trains was authorised on the Down Fast line between the two boxes (only 359 yards apart). Close co-operation between the signalmen at the two junctions and Cock Lane was required to keep traffic moving freely. Ronnie Gee, who was a signalman here in the 1940s, recalls how the Guide Bridge "Pilot" engine, often an N5 tank, from Brookside Sidings would frequently be called upon to Stockport Junction in order to give freight trains (known as "Mossers" bound up the Oldham line for Ashton Moss sidings) a shove up the 1-in-100 towards Crowthorne Junction. Rationalisation in later years completely altered the layout here. The Slow lines between Stockport Junction and Gorton Junction were taken out of use on Sunday, July 2nd.1972. Re-signalling on this stretch began on February 17th.1974 and track removal of the Up SLow line began the following week. The Oldham line round to Crowthorne Junction was closed on May 16th.1983. In the meantime, in July, 1981, the bulk of the Woodhead line-from Hadfield to Penistone-had been abandoned. Stockport Junction signalbox, once such an important link in the trans-Pennine chain, closed on November 16th.1984. *Dr.J.W.Scrimgeour*

Courtesy Signalling Record Society

So concludes this fascinating synopsis of what has been over the years a most intriguing and interesting rail centre. Guide Bridge reached its peak with the widening and developments of the station in the early years of the last century; a feature held in common with the bulk of the British railway network. Decline had begun in June 1930 when the Audenshaw Curve was closed – what a useful connection that would be today! The 1950s saw a renaissance when the Woodhead electrification project was fully opened in 1954. Paradoxically, it was this decade that saw Guide Bridge begin to decline in other directions. Local services over the Fallowfield line had finished in July 1958 and services over the OA&GB to Oldham itself ended the following May.

Passenger services over Woodhead, a feature at Guide Bridge since the line's very inception, ended in January 1970. Through freight lasted longer, but that, too, ended - on July 18th 1981. In the Summer of 1983 at Stockport Junction, where the GCR's census in the early years of the last century had recorded exceptional traffic levels, the layout shrank back to its original two tracks and the quadrupling was no more. Either side of the junction rationalisation had closed Cock Lane signalbox – on January 18th 1970 – with Crowthorne Junction box closing on July 26th of the same year.

In 2012 all signalling at Guide Bridge is in the hands of the Manchester East SCC, though the erstwhile Ashton Junction box still survives. Traffic on and off the Stalybridge branch consists largely of the Class 185 DMUs connecting Manchester Airport with Leeds and the North-East via Manchester Piccadilly. Some freight and the fabled once-weekly (SO) Stockport-Stalybridge train traverse Stockport Junction. Electric services from Piccadilly to Glossop and Hadfield are in the hands of the 3-car Class 323 EMUs. DMUs, including the loathed "Nodding Dogs" (Class 142) ply their trade between Manchester Piccadilly and Marple (Rose Hill) via Hyde. Brookside Sidings, once teeming with all manner of freight, have long been colonised by Network Rail and are used largely for ballast traffic. Guide Bridge, its buildings and surrounding infrastructure laid waste, its once-intensive services removed, has become a microcosm of much of today's railway. However, hope looms on the horizon: over at Stalybridge an intensive re-modelling project prior to the proposed extension of the electrification over the Pennines, has just been completed. We can but remain optimistic!

Lastly, though inevitably we pay much attention to locomotives, trains, stations, signalboxes and the like, it was railwaymen (and women) of all departments and grades that were the life-blood of the railway. Before we leave Guide Bridge we must mention H.W. (Herbert) Ingham who was both yard and station master here for around 30 years until his retirement in the 1960s. Trained as a "Premier" man on the LNER, Herbert lived in the station house at Fairfield and was invariably seen cycling along the trackside cess between his various points of call. His duties covered an area bounded by Fairfield, Ashton Moss and Newton. Described by his former colleagues as something of a gentle giant and with the physique of a "big red-faced farmer", Ingham had a fearsome reputation. Called before a managerial panel to instigate a promotional move, he would have none of it and turned the suggestion down in no uncertain terms; stating that Guide Bridge was where he belonged and would always stay.

Guide Bridge, November 1988: A Class 506 EMU with Driving Trailer Second No. **M59603M** leading pauses at platform 3 en route for Hadfield. Once the pride of the suburban services on the Manchester side of the Woodhead line, these 3-car units were now in the twilight of their service-34 years of continuous work. The spire of St.Stephen's church on Guide Lane gives an unmistakable clue to our location. Stockport Junction box and the line down towards Denton Junction and Reddish South can just be glimpsed in the background. *W.A.Brown*

Guide Bridge Station, n.d: One of J.G.Robinson's renowned and sturdy Class 9N (LNER A5) 4-6-2 Tank locomotives, No.**371** is seen at the west end of platform 4 with an express working. The first coach of the train is one of Robinson's celebrated "Barnum" vehicles. Built in 1910 these highly distinctive carriages had straight sides, matchboard panelling and recessed end doors. The train, facing towards Manchester, stands adjacent to the end of Cock Lane sidings; Guide Lane crosses the railway at right-angles. The wagon in the background carries the name of John Mellor & Sons, coal and coke factors here at Guide Bridge. No.371 was turned out of Gorton in June 1917 and was withdrawn in July 1957. *P.F.Cooke*

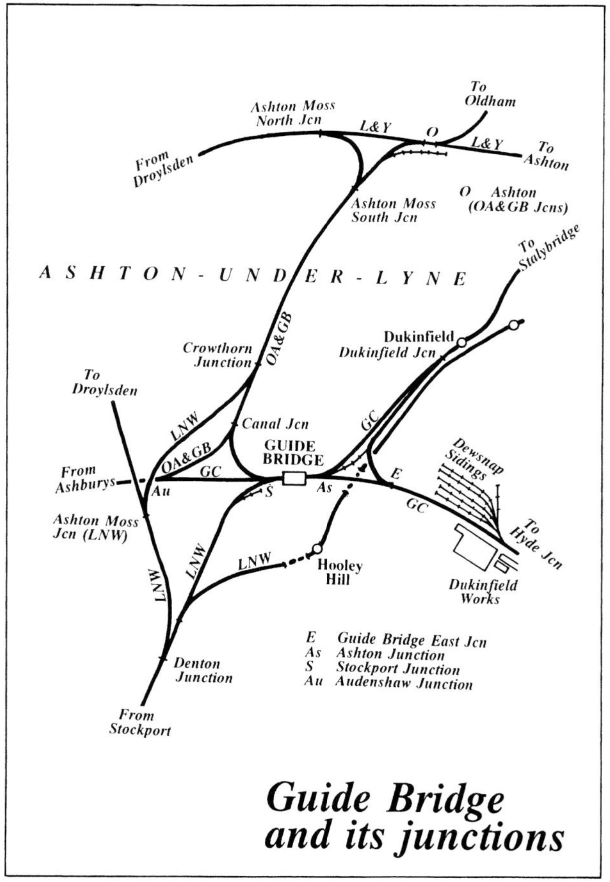

Guide Bridge and its junctions

Guide Bridge c.1919: This is what suburban workings in and out of Manchester over the Great Central main line looked like in the immediate post-World War I period. Class 3 (LNER F1) 2-4-2 Tank No.**731** waits alongside platform 2 with a stopping train bound for Manchester London Road. Comprised of gas-lit 6-wheeled carriages, commuters would have been assured of a bumpy ride and a smoothness far removed from the electric stock which came onstream with the 1954 modernisation programme. The hoarding by the lattice staircase to the footbridge proclaims the sale of Government factories by private treaty-an indication that hostilities had ceased and the great conflict was finally over. *P.F.Cooke*

Guide Bridge, n.d: Class 3 (F1) 2-4-2 Tank No.**730** has arrived at platform 3 with an Up local working. The train has run into Guide Bridge along the Up Slow line and may have originated from Manchester Central, travelling via the Fallowfield line. No.730 carries a Belpaire boiler which it had received in December 1913. What a pretty sight these splendid-looking little engines must have been in their rich Great Central Brunswick green, lined out black and white. Though the 2-4-2 genre was largely ousted by the later, more powerful Robinson 4-4-2 Tanks, No.730 lasted until November 1944. Notice the unusual positioning of the signal spanning the tracks between the station awnings.

Author's collection

Electrification of the Woodhead Route was not simply confined to the former GCR main line between Manchester London Road and Sheffield Victoria. Tied in with the scheme was a myriad of sundry sidings, yards and feeder lines. Perforce, part of the project included, the OA&GB line from Stockport Junction as far as Ashton Moss South Junction.

Crowthorne Junction, Manchester Road, September 28th 1953: Overhead masts are creeping down from Ashton Moss South, but as yet have no catenary. Were it not for bridges, the electrification of railways would be a simpler task. Bridge No.7 which carried Manchester Road (A635) over the OA&GB line needed rebuilding and its clearances increasing for the overhead catenary. The official photographer recorded this rather fine view of a structure which had been in situ since 1861. With stone abutments and buttresses, the bridge had cast iron girders and stone flag flooring. The photographer has his back to Crowthorne Junction; the splitting Home arms protect the line to Stockport Junction and round to the right (behind the camera) to Ashton Moss Junction on the Denton line, respectively. Overhead electrification of a different kind is seen along Manchester Road in the shape of trolleybus wires for the 218 and 219 services that plied this route. *British Railways*

September 28th 1953: For the reconstruction it was necessary to close Manchester Road piecemeal, one half at a time. This picture, looking in the opposite direction, shows the nature and complexity of the job in hand; bear in mind that trains had to be kept running while the rebuilding went on. Engineers have removed the roadway on the north side and are, possibly, awaiting a weekend possession to remove the old cast iron girders. Notice the shower of debris on the track; doubtless today the HSE would require safety netting to be in place, or maybe a complete line closure would be considered. Crowthorne Junction signalbox is tucked out of sight on the left behind the adjacent bridge – another stone arch structure from the same period. *British Railways*

Crowthorne Junction, c.1964: Electrification over this section of the OA&GB is now finished. Looking north to Ashton Moss South Junction this was Crowthorne Junction; the former LNWR Denton and Crowthorne line to Stockport via Ashton Moss and Denton junctions veers away to the left of the picture. Prior to electrification, in 1947, Crowthorne Junction worked to Ashton Moss Colliery box on this line. New Moss Colliery, with its array of sidings, stood on the site of what is today's Snipe Retail Park. Crowthorne Junction was a Saxby and Farmer box and housed a rocker frame designed by that company. The very lofty nature of the box was a requirement to enable sighting over the numerous overbridges adjacent to the junction. Ahead of the box is the bridge taking Crowthorne Lane over the railway. In January 1954, to avoid rebuilding, a temporary overbridge was installed with wooden parapets. Beyond this bridge can be seen the reconstructed Manchester Road bridge, now complete with pre-stressed concrete girders. The "overhead" is wired and the Bo+Bos will soon be trundling up and down to and from Ashton Moss South exchange sidings with "The Mossers". Rationalisation here saw the Up and Down lines exchange names (from March 23rd 1969). Crowthorne Junction box was closed on July 26th 1970 and its functions transferred to Ashton Moss South. Subsequently, the line from here to Stockport Junction was closed as well - on May 16th 1983.
Dr.J.W.F.Scrimgeour/SRS

Ashton Moss South Junction, April 17th 1956: Ashton Moss sidings, together with the north-westerly curve to the L&Y's Ashton Branch, were opened by the GCR in December 1911. The sidings were grouped in two sets: a set of 14 with two through roads at the top, running parallel with the Ashton Branch. The group could be accessed from Ashton Moss North on the west side and over towards OA&GB Junction to the east. The second set, sited alongside the easterly curve from Ashton Moss South to the Ashton Branch, was arranged as a set of 12 loops thus providing access from both ends. In the photograph the train of plate wagons in the foreground is waiting on the curve which runs round to join the Ashton Branch at Ashton Moss North Junction. Permissive block working was in use here – an indication of the level of traffic at one time. The train of containers and goods vans stands on the long siding which ran round from the L&Y line adjacent to the curve. In the background, the mineral wagons stand on the sidings by the Ashton Branch. The plume of steam seen to the far right is from a loco busy in Ashton Oldham Road goods yard close the easterly connecting curve to the Ashton Branch at Ashton West Junction. Behind the curve stand buildings belonging to The National Gas Engine Company whose premises extended for some distance alongside the Down line here. In 2012 the scene at Ashton Moss has changed out of all recognition. The 1911 curve to Ashton Moss North still exists and has even seen an LMS "Duchess" pass along this summer (2012). A large Sainsbury's supermarket now covers the site across to the ex-L&Y line where the eastern curve and exchange sidings once stood. The supermarket is accessed from a new road – Lord Sheldon Way – which carries the new Metrolink extension off Manchester Road into Ashton town centre. New rails for old at 21st century Ashton Moss. *Dr.J.W.F.Scrimgeour/Courtesy Signalling Record Society*

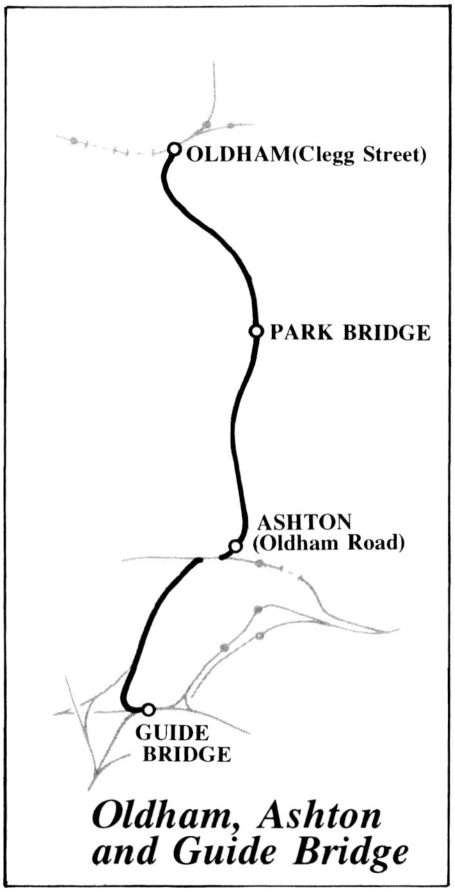

Ashton Moss South Junction, March 31st 1974: A view showing the signalbox and the now grassy void where the exchange sidings used to be. The picture is taken from the Richmond Street overbridge (Bridge No.10) and looks north to the ex-L&Y line seen running across the top of the picture in front of the white-painted houses. Off to the left is the 1911 curve connecting the OA&GB with the L&Y's Ashton Branch at Ashton Moss North Junction. Notice the curve has lost its overhead line, though supporting masts still stand. Similarly, the Up loop and east curve in front of the box have been de-electrified, too. In 1953 trials were carried out here with an experimental design of tubular overhead mast. An all-welded product of Tubewrights Ltd., it was stated that the design could withstand a 250% excess load in winds of 50 mph. Interestingly, a similar design has been used on today's Metrolink extensions and can be seen a mere stone's throw away at the new Ashton Moss tram stop. The east curve to OA&GB Junction from Ashton Moss South Junction was closed on December 22nd 1991 along with the signalbox which was left in situ and "mothballed". In early Spring of 1996 it was destroyed in an arson attack; the 70-lever RSC tappet frame survived the fire but was later removed. Today the only remaining feature of this once-busy site is the redundant 3-arm bracket signal which controlled the junction on the Up line. This can be seen from the car park at what is today the Ashton Moss Leisure Park below Lord Sheldon Way. Across the line, part of The National Gas Engine's factory still stands staring at names like Cine World, Frankie & Benny's, Chibuito and Hollywood Bowl. All a part of the modern culture that has seen the total eclipse of railway features such as this. *M.A.King*

OA&GB Junction, August 1956: Fairburn 2-6-4 Tank No.**42115** has travelled up from Stockport Edgeley with the 12.34 (SO) train to Oldham. From Stockport the train will have left the LNWR main line at Heaton Norris Junction. Continuing through Reddish (South) and Denton 42115 will have taken the left fork at Denton Junction onto the Guide Bridge Junction line. At Ashton Moss Junction the service headed off in a north-easterly direction through the district of Audenshaw. Off to the left, between the railway and Manchester Road, was the New Moss Colliery complete with rail access and a number of sidings. Today this is the site of the Snipe Retail Park which houses such names as B&Q and MFI with no trace whatever of the railway. At Crowthorne Junction LNWR territory became OA&GB; the train would have passed under Manchester Road and then on towards Ashton Moss South Junction before turning away to briefly join the L&Y line at a point just under the bridge in the background. In our view the train has just left the L&Y line and is back on OA&GB tracks en route for Oldham. The signalbox at OA&GB Junction controlled what was, in effect, two junctions. Ashton West Junction runs off to the left under the occupation bridge by the signalbox; beyond here is Ashton Moss South Junction and the exchange sidings. 42115 has just negotiated Ashton East Junction where, as mentioned, the Oldham line commences. The former L&Y main line (Ashton Branch) continues ahead under the bridge towards Manchester Victoria via Ashton Moss North Junction and Droylsden. *Jim Davenport*

Ashton, Oldham Road, August 1956: A pretty scene with the station garden seen in full bloom enhanced by carefully-painted rockery pieces and the station's name diligently worked in the banking in stones. When plastic-coated steel and perspex make do for station accommodation today, we can only gaze on sights like this, with the quasi-pagoda waiting shelter and beautiful MS&L-style gas lamps in awe. Fairburn 2-6-4 Tank is paying its usual early afternoon call with the 12.42 (SO) Oldham Clegg Street to Stockport train. The train was due in Stockport at 1.09 which included a stop at the now long-closed Heaton Norris station on the fringe of Stockport town centre. Notice the engineering manufactory of Messrs.Joshua Heap with name and business title emblazoned on the gable wall. Typical of today's industries in and around Ashton-under-Lyne, it is good to know that Joshua Heap is still with us-alive and well on Boodle Street. *Jim Davenport*

Park Bridge Station, April 1959: Looking south towards Ashton and Guide Bridge, we see a somewhat seedy-looking station in the last few weeks of its existence; for closure was effected the following month. The uneven nature of the platforms is noticeable, owing no doubt to the subsidence due to colliery workings in the immediate vicinity. *Donald Cash*

Park Bridge Viaduct, June 1954: The multi-storey mill building provides us with definite clues to our location-the outskirts of Oldham, long famed as one of the principal Lancashire cotton towns. Stanier 2-6-4 Tank No.**42551** is crossing Park Bridge viaduct with the 12.27 (SO) Greenfield to Stockport train. The four or so miles from Greenfield, which lay on the LNWR's Manchester to Huddersfield main line, took the train via Grasscroft, Grotton and Springhead, Lees and two Oldham stations, both Glodwick Road and Clegg Street before emerging onto the viaduct here. The route to Stockport would have been the reverse of No.42115 in the earlier picture. Park Bridge viaduct seemed to have a promising future when, in 1960, it was refurbished to accommodate an expected upturn in traffic originating from Oldham's Clegg Street parcels depot. Sadly, this was not to be and this stately-looking stone structure was demolished in 1971. *Jim Davenport*

Oldham, Glodwick Road, n.d: I felt that the section covering the OA&GB would not have been complete without I included this superb period view of the northernmost outpost of the system. Here a GCR Class 3 tank engine No.**576** (LNER Class F1) has run round its train prior to travelling bunker-first back to Guide Bridge via Oldham Clegg Street. The ride in the rake of six LNWR 6-wheeled coaches would, one feels, have been interesting!
Ray Webster/W.A.Brown collection

Guide Bridge Station, July 6th.1933: A somewhat serener scene is portrayed by this study of former Great Central Atlantic No.**6086** about to move off eastwards with an express. While present-day enthusiasts will marvel at scenes like this: a splendidly-proportioned Edwardian express engine, albeit painted black, at the head of a train of teak-bodied coaching stock-the official seen walking down the ramp on the left seems unconcerned; and why should he be anything else? Such sights were par for the course at the time and would have been scarcely worth a second glance by staff who gazed upon scenes like this around the clock 365 days a year. Will future generations breath sighs at the sight of Class 305 EMUs, 158s and Sprinters? *Author's collection*

Guide Bridge, East End of Station, c.1923: One of J.G.Robinson's 8G 4-6-0s (LNER B9) No.**1110** pulls away from Guide Bridge with an Up Express. Built by Beyer, Peacock & Co. in 1906 this class of 10 4-6-0s with 5'-4" coupled wheels was essentially a smaller-wheeled version of the somewhat better-known "Immingham" Class express goods engine produced by Beyer, Peacock earlier in the year. No.1110 cvarries the Great Central's black goods livery, lined red and white. *Author's collection*

Guide Bridge Station, East End, c.1924: An unusual working, by today's standards, passes a familiar spot. An immaculate-looking Robinson Class D9 (LNER 11D) 4-4-0 No.**6034** runs through Guide Bridge with the Manchester London Road portion of the through Hull-Liverpool Express. The two coaches seen here were detached at Godley Junction; the remainder of the train then continued its journey to Liverpool Central via Stockport Tiviot Dale and Glazebrook. The fine lattice (public) footbridge spanned both the goods yard and main lines. Numbered 25 in the Guide Bridge register, it comprises three spans: 95'-0" and 89'-8" over the goods yard and 95'-5" over the running lines. Bridge 25 has cast-iron columns and brick abutments; the lattice girders are of steel; construction dates from c.1900. No.6034 had been built by Sharp, Stewart in 1902. She was withdrawn in November, 1949. *Author's collection*

Guide Bridge Station, East End, c.1946/47: The East end of Guide Bridge station was a favourite vantage point for photographers over the years from pre-Grouping up to modern times. An uncluttered, easily accessed vantage point enhanced by a splendid array of semaphore signals with a wide variety of trains and motive power have provided us with a veritable feast of scenes. Here is one such: K3 2-6-0 No.**1808** makes a splendid spectacle as she blasts away from platform 3 with an Up express. Notice the semaphores bear a family likeness to those at Ashburys, Priory Junction and Gorton Station. No.1808 had begun life at Doncaster, as a member of Great Northern Class H4 in July, 1921. She had been variously 1008, 4008, 1808 and 61808. In this latter guise she was withdrawn from service in September 1961. *W.H. Whitworth.*

Guide Bridge Station, May 26th.1956: The crew of 04/8 No.**63794** gaze intently at the photographer as their short freight train drifts along the Up Slow line past platform 1. Behind the rather fine canopy, St.Stephen's church, a landmark on many railway photographs taken in this area, casts its spire up towards the clear summer sky. *B.K.B.Green*

Guide Bridge Station, view from East End, 1955: Another unique photograph from the series of cab views used to illustrate the route between Manchester London Road and Shefield Victoria. The train is traversing the Down Fast line and will shortly come to rest alongside platform 4 at a point roughly where the picture of the Class 506 EMU was taken. Our photograph gives some idea of the complexity of the station layout in the immediate post-electrification years. An electric loco hides in the cattle dock behind platform 4, over to the left. Guide Bridge was a watering and feeding station for cattle trains under the watchful eye of Paddy Galvin, an Inspector. Charges were raised for feeding and watering per head of cattle. In this period, rates were 1/6d-1/10d per beast; much of the station's cattle movement was in Irish traffic. A Special Traffic notice indicated the arrival of trains, splitting and re-marshalling then being done as necessary. Beyond the Cattle Dock, the red brick two-storey building housed the station offices and dated from the widening programme which commenced in 1903 and brought about the subsequent enlargement of the station to its present state. Looking over the panorama notice the double slips at the near end of platform 3 to enable movements to and from both far and near running lines to platform 4. The line cutting in from the left is the Down Goods No.2, a loop that could be accessed at both Hyde Junction and Guide Bridge East boxes further down the line. This line led also into the shunting neck which terminated in the cattle dock shown on the photo. *B.K.B.Green*

Guide Bridge, c.1951: A lattice bridge "Grandstand" view as B17 No.61643 *Champion Lodge* leaves platform 1 and takes the Stalybridge line at Ashton Junction – notice the "peg" is off with Guide Bridge North's distant beneath. The train is the 5.40 pm Manchester London Road to Stalybridge, a service often used for running-in locos ex-works from Gorton – notice No.61643's pristine condition. Over in Brookside sidings all manner of freight stock, line upon line of wagons and vans clutter the various roads. To the left can be seen the two coaches of the Oldham push-pull set. The sidings today are reduced to holding Engineering trains for Network Rail. And more change is on the way with the recent announcement that the route to Stalybridge and Leeds is to be electrified. But 60 years ago a veritable panorama of mills, chimneys and industry galore provided a backdrop to this, an ever-fascinating railway scene. *Geoff Parrish*

Guide Bridge, early 1950s: Darnall's K3 No.61848 basks in glorious sunshine while getting easily to grips with an Up express leaving platform 3. The picture is taken from that splendid lattice overbridge here at Guide Bridge's east end. Notice the mill buildings in the background; these belonged to Guide Mills on Kershaw Street, just one of the many such in the area that had provided employment for generations of locals and, of course, traffic for the railway. Don't miss the MS&L 6-wheeled coach body behind the loco; a full brake, it was still there before the war, a remarkable hangover from early GCR days. Inside the impressive goods shed were two cranes: 12cwt at the west and 30cwt at the east end. To the left of the warehouse is the two-storey office building. Pointing skywards in the background can be seen the spire belonging to St.Stephen's church. Standing on the corner of Guide Lane and Audenshaw Road, the church is a local landmark and features on many pictures of the station.

Geoff Parrish

Ashton Junction, April 19th.1956: A view looking east from the end of platform 1. This was Ashton Junction which, along with Stockport Junction, was one of the main nerve centres on this part of the Woodhead line. The sidings across on the right were known as the "Liverpool Sidings", Brookside Sidings lie over to the left, beyond the goods shed and the lattice footbridge. Further down the line the branch to Stalybridge curves away towards Guide Bridge North Junction. It was the fragmentation of the various goods facilities here that was advanced, inter alia, as one of the reasons for the building of Mottram Yard. *Dr.J.W.F. Scrimgeour courtesy Signalling Record Society*

Guide Bridge n.d: A view at the east end of the station proving the point that the Great Central didn't have all the train workings around these parts to themselves and revealing the joint nature of some of the lines in and around this nerve centre. The engine (number unknown) is one of George Whale's "19 in. Express Goods" 4-6-0s which dated from the end of 1906. A 5'-2 1/2"-wheeled version of the same designer's "Experiments", the engines were intended for fast goods trains and slower passenger services. The appearance of this specimen, engaged in shunting two coal wagons and a cattle wagon, therefore, seems a trifle strange. *W.H. Whitworth.*

Dukinfield Central, March 20th.1952: Located at the west end of Wharf Street and utilising Station Street as its "subway", Dukinfield Central served trains on the Stalybridge branch from Guide Bridge until its demise in 1959. It is thought that the station here dated from 1862 replacing a more basic facility situated a few yards to the east. The manner in which the viaduct at this point was widened supports this theory. Opened in 1845, two days before Christmas, the line crossed the Peak Forest Canal close to the junction with the Huddersfield Canal at Portland basin. The canal bridge itself was a graceful structure comprising six cast iron arched girders. Creation of the station's platforms over the canal resulted in additional support in the form of wrought iron plate girders which duly hid the decorative cast facias from sight. Dukinfield Central had stone buildings on both platforms, access being from Station Street via a series of stone steps which survived until reconstruction of the bridge in later years. This view from the Guide Bridge direction reveals an extremely neat and tidy station with fixtures and fittings that reveal the station's Great Central ancestry. Victorian artefacts such as cast iron lamp standards-those beautiful MS&L bases again-and platform seating convey a feeling of antiquity associated with our railway system until comparatively recent times. In pre-Group days, Dukinfield Central enjoyed a service of upwards of a dozen trains in each direction, mostly between the towns of Stockport and Stalybridge. There were occasional through workings to and from Manchester London Road and Oldham with travelling times certainly comparable with those of their successors. *British Railways*

Dukinfield Central, March 20th.1952: This view, taken from the canal towpath, illustrates some traditional industries in decline. Although not the weed-choked channels they were soon to become, the days of the canals were now numbered. The stockpiles of earthenware pipes, drains and chimney pots lining the canal side were products of Messrs.John Hall, a long-established company in the area. Sadly, Halls were to succumb in 1967. Closure of Dukinfield Central ultimately resulted in the removal of both platforms and buildings. Note that the plate girders seen here reveal, once again, the cast iron structure of 1845. Subsequent reconstruction of this bridge, in 1979, retained something of its originality by the exposure of the external face of the cast iron member following encasement in concrete. *British Railways*

Ashton Junction, looking east, n.d: Class C13 4-4-2 Tank No.**67416** heads east towards Dewsnap Sidings and Hyde Junction with a push-pull working on the Manchester London Road to Glossop service. Both running lines and siding space reflect the intensity of the traffic once worked through here. The photographer is standing on the lattice footbridge seen in the D9 picture; Ashton Junction signalbox stands on the right, behind the footbridge. Up and Down Slow lines are over to the left where the light engine is positioned. The junction for the Stalybridge line is immediately ahead. Next to these lines are Up Fast, on which the Local is travelling, and Down Fast respectively. Peeping out behind the push-pull unit is a G2 0-8-0 on the old Down No.1 Loop. To the right of these is the complex known as the "Liverpool Sidings". Astley Street bridge spans the tracks in the background along with mill chimneys and terraced houses once so much a part, almost a stereotype, of Northern England.

Jim Davenport

Guide Bridge East Junction 9th.February, 1952: Though the Woodhead line climbed almost steadily from Manchester London Road to just past milepost 21, about three-quarters of the way through Woodhead Tunnel itself, through Guide Bridge station the route is level past Ashton Junction. A brief interruption at 1-in-170 occurs, levelling again before climbing sharply at 1-in-77 towards Guide Bridge East. Here the curve of 1906 is encountered which linked in with the Stalybridge line at Guide Bridge North Junction. Making heavy weather up this gradient is 04/7 No.**63761** with a returning train of coal empties for the Yorkshire pits. These impressive-looking, if ugly, machines were a rebuild (from 1938 on) of the original handsome Robinson 8K 2-8-0 design dating from 1912.

B.K.B.Green

Dewsnap Sidings, May 9th. 1953. B1 No.**61183** passes the west end of the yard with Astley Street (at one time known as "Astley Lane" or "Dog Lane")-bridge No.30 in the background. The train is the 12.50 p.m. ex Liverpool (Central) to Harwich Boat train which the B1 would have brought from Manchester Central along the Fallowfield line. Behind the railed perimeter fence is the former Dukinfield Carriage and Wagon Works. The lofty semaphores were electro-pneumatically operated. On the right of the gantry, the small arm controlled the junction ahead at Guide Bridge East where the curve to the Stalybridge Branch via Guide Bridge North Junction ran off. *B.K.B. Green.*

DEWSNAP SIDINGS

Little more than a passing reference has been made to Dewsnap Sidings in previous books dealing with the Woodhead line; something which seems strange given the key role that the complex played in the workings of freight traffic over the line.

Dewsnap Sidings were sited just three quarters of a mile east of Guide Bridge station and were located almost equi-distant between Guide Bridge East and Hyde Junctions on the north side of the GCR main line. Dating from around the mid-1860s the complex grew as focal interchange point for freight traffic on the western side of the Woodhead route. On the south side of the line and facing the complex, the Great Central had built their Dukinfield carriage and wagon works which opend in 1910.

The exact history of the Dewsnap complex is imprecise and not at all clear. A small wagon repair depot had existed at Dog Lane, site of the first Dukinfield station. Dow reports this works as having closed in 1861 and the work transferred to Gorton. An OS map first surveyed in 1872 and later re-surveyed in 1891-92, shows a small complex of sidings with the name "Dog Lane Siding" on the site of the much bigger yard. Dog Lane was later re-titled "Astley Street" but the name seems to have stuck. These early sidings consisted of 14 roads and a small wagon works which stood behind Turner Street and opposite the Stanley Wood Cotton Mill. The sidings also served Astley Deep Pit, to the west of King Street and part of the Dukinfield Collieries. On the south side of the line was the Dewsnap Pit which doubtless gave the later sidings their name.

The 1872 map shows a tramway connecting the Astley and Dewsnap pits. This was carried via a bridge over the railway-about 250 yards west of the King Street overbridge (numbered 31). Both pits were swept away with the enlargement of the sidings and the creation of Dukinfield Carriage and Wagon Works. Certainly, no record of the tramway bridge exists in the Guide Bridge district bridge register which was culled from early LNER records. The yard proper is likely to have dated from around 1875 when two goods lines were installed between Guide Bridge and what Dow refers to as "Dewsnap Junction." This latter was probably at Dewsnap Bridge (King Street, No.31) where the line from the Astley Deep Pit joined the main line. The early map shows some confirmation of this in the form of a signalbox here.

In modern times the total wagon handling capacity at Dewsnap was recorded as being 2,431. Traffic was handled in four main groups of sidings (56 in all) laid parallel to the running lines. Three reception sidings were housed between the through (running) lines and the complex of sidings themselves. Up and Down main lines were sandwiched between Down Goods No.1 on the north side and Down Goods No.2 on the south side. At peak times of operation the Up Goods line was pressed into use as an additional reception road.

Each siding had its own reference according to the traffic it carrried. This traffic, most of it originating from the west side of the country included limestone and general merchandise as well. Six shunting necks at the east end of the complex aided the sorting process; the sidings were all "dead ends"-there being no through running at Dewsnap. A peculiarity was the odd names given to the various siding groups. The southern group (nearest to the main line) was known as Dog Lane (from the site of the wagon repair shop) and housed wagons for local traders and Stockport goods yard. No.2 group sidings (1-6) were referred to as "Kelly", 7-14 as "Klondyke" and No.15 were known as "Back Slip." A further group of sidings to the east of the yard, which ran at an angle of about 45 degrees to the main group, were used to service a rail storage facility. Behind this small cluster of siding roads was a wagon repair shop. This, under an agreement first dated April 8th.1926, was leased to Wagon Repairs Limited. Other activity on this side of Dewsnap centred around R.J.Coley & Sons Jubilee scrap metal works which fringed onto the land here, adjacent to what was then a cricket field. Latterly, the Chief Civil Engineer was responsible for these subsidiary sidings which handled ballast traffic; 242 wagons could be housed here in total.

Two signalboxes controlled entry to and from the yard: Guide Bridge East from the west side and Dewsnap Sidings box from the east. Dewsnap box controlled all the movements in and out of the various shunting necks and movements over the crossovers; exits were in the direction of Hyde Junction. All points beyind the sorting roads were hand-operated, something that must have made operation laborious to say the very least. Ken Ainsworth, a signalman here for several years, spoke to me of the intense activity inside the box which precluded signalmen from taking a meal break. A grumble of the signalmen was that the shunters did appear at least to be able to snatch a 20 minute respite.

In common with many railway sites where round-the-clock activity ruled the day, staff housing was provided near the sidings. Ken Ainsworth recalls that 12 or so such dwellings were provided for Inspectors by "the company" on Astley Street, a main thoroughfare which ran from Globe Square-just near to Dukinfield Works-along the back of the sidings. Runaway wagons banging into the stopblocks at the end of the siding roads would frequently disturb the populace in the small hours!

Dewsnap was not a modern purpose-built yard on the "hump" principle. The foreman shunter might call up to the box "Klondyke, Bobby!" indicating to which group of sidings wagons were to be sent. As wagons were propelled from the shunting necks back into the yard, their destinations within the siding group was signalled to the shunters or "chasers" who would then be required to run alongside the speeding vehicles and jam a stick under the brake lever to arrest the speed. Small wonder that accidents to shunters were frequent; such movements must have called for an almost athletic ability as feet jumped over rails and crossings in rain, fog, snow and frost. A shunter's lot at Dewsnap, or anywhere else for that matter, cannot have been a happy one.

Dewsnap Sidings, September 23rd.1956: Looking west towards Guide Bridge this is a splendid panorama, a scene captured in oneof the rare moments when both the main line and the sidings were quiet. Sat in the middle of the plethora of running lines and siding roads is the signalbox-a Class 1 box which did not directly serve the running lines! Looking left to right seven running lines stretch from the boundary of Dukinfield Works (just visible far left) to the front of the box; these are: Down Goods (2), Down Main, Up Main, Down Goods (1), Up Goods, No.1 Loop, No.2 Loop. A third loop (designated No.3 Loop) connected from the Stalybridge Branch at Guide Bridge East-to where the various groups of sidings stretched-and made a connection with the entry and exit roads from the first two groups of sidings.On the photographer's right, the calling-on arm is "off" for the Up Goods line from here to Hyde Junction. Through the thicket of "Overhead" the outline of two Bo-Bos is just discernible. After the closure of the Woodhead route the need for Dewsnap Sidings and its associated signalbox ceased; the box was abolished officially on March 4th.1984. The forest of overhead catenary with its copper contact wire was cut up on the spot and sold to a German company for scrap. Perhaps the ultimate irony for part of a project that had been the pride of the post-WWII British Railway system.

Dewsnap Sidings Signalbox, September 23rd.1956: The interior of Dewsnap Sidings box caught in a lull between the bouts of frenetic activity that appear to have been commonplace here throughout the working day. As mentioned in the text, Dewsnap did not control movements on the main line but was confined to controlling traffic to and from Guide Bridge East and Hyde Junction and in and out of the various groups of siding roads. Above the "frame" with its 40 pull-out slides for operating the various points and signals can be seen the indicator lights for normal and reversed operation. On the suspended shelf sit two block bells and block instruments with indicators for permissive block working over the various goods lines. Above the window can be seen several "clips"-screwed clamps for locking points when working "wrong line". Next to these is a pair of pressure gauges: these recorded the air pressure available to operate the points and signals: 28 lb. psi for the former, 15lb. psi for the latter. An oil lamp seems to be the only source of illumination above the frame; a statutory hand lamp sits just behind slide No.40. *Dr.J. W.F.Scrimgeour/courtesy Signalling Record Society*

Dewsnap Sidings, May 9th.1953: A mention of the name *Flying Scotsman* these days is sufficent to bring out a vast throng of the enthusiast fraternity complete with a plethora of cameras and video recorders. Only Brian Green and his trusty Zeiss Ikon were out on this May afternoon to photograph what was then merely A3 Pacific No.**60103** at the head of the 3.50 pm Manchester to Marylebone Express. Notice the world's most famous steam locomotive is still driven from the right: left-hand drive was not effected until April, 1954. *B.K.B.Green*

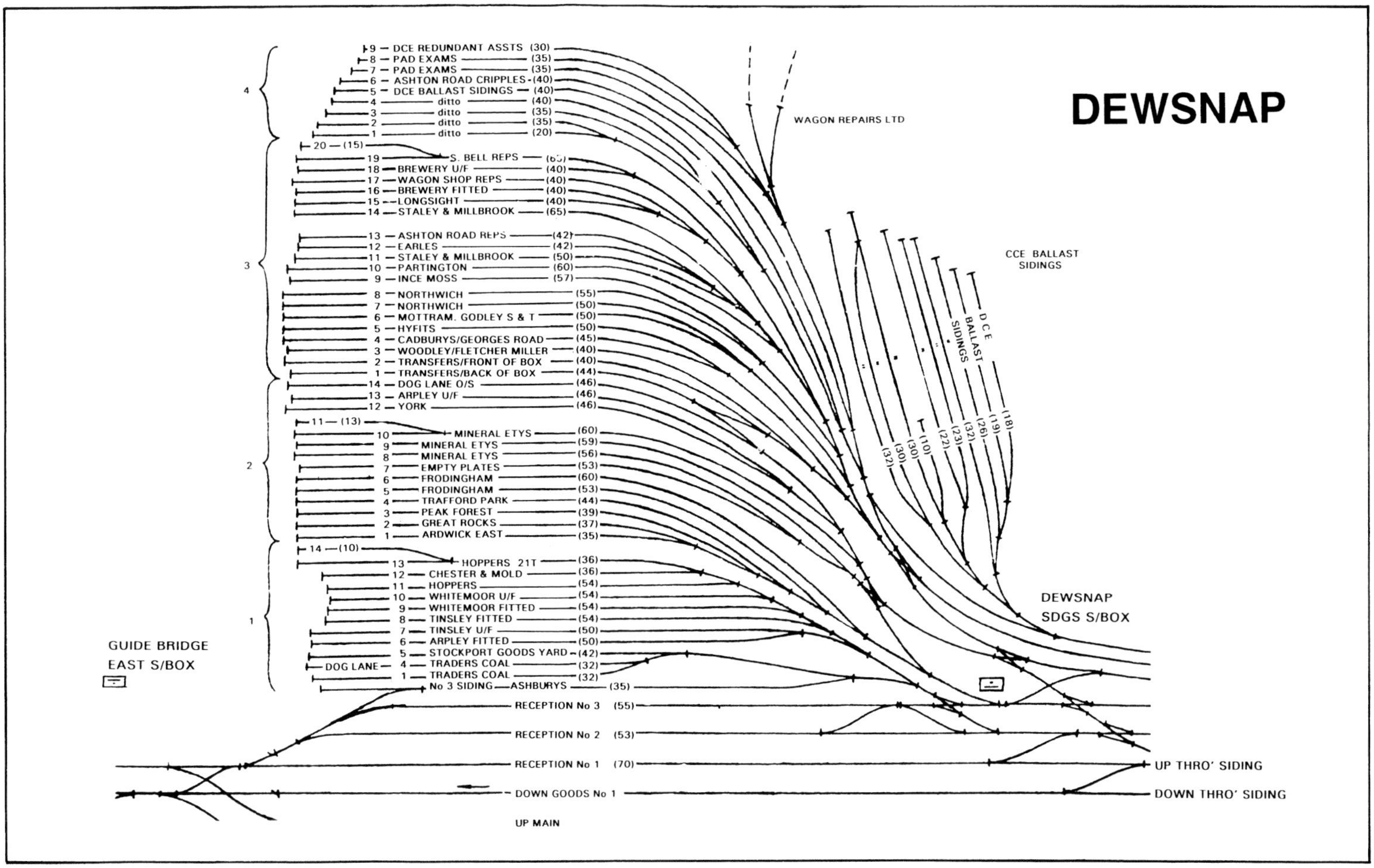

Dewsnap Sidings, April 12th.1954: Gresley's massive Garratt 2-8-8-2 Class U1 had spent much of its early and middle life banking coal trains up the Worsborough incline on the line between Penistone and Wath. Our picture shows the mammoth at Dewsnap sidings in its oil-fired state; conversion from coal firing having taken place in 1952. Some kind of test working is in progress; the previous October No.**69999** had worked a train of 43 wagons, a load of around 600 tons, from here to Crowden and back again. At this period in its career, the Garratt is recorded at having been in Gorton Works for what are termed "non-classified repairs." After a somewhat mixed post-war career Britain's most powerful steam locomotive was withdrawn in December, 1955. It was cut up at Doncaster in the early part of 1956. *B.K.B.Green*

Dewsnap Sidings, n.d: An uneventful scene at Dewsnap Sidings; a shot taken from a train standing on the Down Goods line. By the looks of things a possession for permanent way work is in force. Shunter Joe Catherole, mug of tea in hand, gesticulates as a pair of bogie bolster wagons is set back along No.2 Reception road towards the yard. Vision on the Up Goods No.1 line is partially obscured as a torrent of steam erupts from the cylinders of an 8F 2-8-0. Dewsnap Sidings box, set back on the right, housed 28 levers. Working on the electro-pneumatic system the box was concerned with workings in and out of the yard and did not signal trains along the main line. The block section proper extended from Guide Bridge East to Hyde Junction. *Ken Ainsworth*

Dukinfield Works pre-WWI: A general view of the west end of the works taken from the roof of the main building. We are looking in a north-westerly direction; the main offices bearing the legend "Great Central Railway Co. Carriage and Wagon Dept." is proudly emblazoned over the entrance door. The 100,00 gallon water tank sits on stilts behind; beyond, through the haze, can just be made out the signals (which show on our picture of B1 No.61183) controlling the main line which passed the back of the works. In the foreground is a scene packed with interest: wagons, all lettered "GC" or "CL", fill the siding roads. Wheelsets, in serried rows, are lined up with military precision-doubtless for the photograph. Behind are the rails where the traverser runs enabling wagons from any road to be brought to and from any part of the shops with speed and ease. Notice the lovely little Saloon coach in the foreground with the white roof. This is Lettered "GCR C&W Dept. Dukinfield" and is almost certainly some kind of inspection vehicle. Part of the Iron Store, used in later years as an electrical assembly shop, projects from the right-hand side of the scene.

National Railway Museum

THE DUKINFIELD CARRIAGE & WAGON WORKS OF THE GCR

The cramped nature of the environment at Gorton, coupled with the impossibility of extending the existing works there, led the GCR's management to select a site for a new carriage and wagon works at Dukinfield, Cheshire. This was situated ½ a mile east of Guide Bridge station and faced Dewsnap sidings across the main line. Spacious accommodation was available to the company at Dukinfield and the chosen site covered 27½ acres. The land had been previously occupied by the Dukinfield Colliery and the site was purchased by the GCR on April 19th.1904 from A.C.Boyd and a Mrs.Nicholson.

Contractors for the work were Messrs.Craven Bros.Ltd. of Manchester and Messrs.Markham & Co.Ltd. of Chesterfield. A budget of £165,000 was allowed for the new works. On top of this, a further sum of almost £20,000 was set aside for a power station within the complex.

Work began on the site early in 1906. On completion of the various buildings, machine tools and equipment used for carriage and wagon building at Gorton were transferred to the new premises. These were supplemented by a number of modern high-speed machine tools; the company seemingly determined to put production on the most rapid and economical footing possible. Production at Dukinfield is reported as having commenced in 1908, with full output being achieved by the end of 1910.

The works buildings consisted of two main clusters: the smaller group, at the east end of the site, was utilised for carriage repair and lifting; the larger group-at the west end-was used for carriage and wagon building and repair work. Plentiful siding space was provided and the works was connected at either end to the main line. A key feature within the complex was the electric traverser which served the whole width of the shops. This was 66 ft. long and had a carrying capacity of 45 tons at 5 miles per hour. Vehicles were hauled on and off the traverser by a capstan with a speed of 200 ft. per minute.

The main entrance to the works was near the west end of Globe Lane. Workers, there were no less than around 1,400 of them initially (including some girls who were employed as upholsterers), entered the complex via a 1-in-15 slope rising towards the lodge and mess room. Study of this building makes for a fascinating insight into the industrial practices of the time. Covering an area of 200 ft. by 50 ft., the mess room was divided into three sections: one housed up to 1,100 men, another 40 foremen and clerical staff and third housed a kitchen complete with gas ovens, grills and hot water boilers. Workmen using the mess room deposited their baskets on arrival before entering the lodge where they collected a "check" which they kept for the day and handed it back before leaving. "Clocking in" was then accomplished. Newspapers were provided in the mess room and items of daily news were read out to the men during their lunch interval. This was in contrast to a practice pertaining once upon a time at Derby Locomotive Works where scripture readings during meal times were the order of the day!

The main block of shops comprised an area some 700 ft.long and 540 ft.wide. On the east side was a timber yard, above this a timber drying shed was situated. This led immediately inside to the saw mill-all part of a heavy reliance on the use of timber and reflecting the wagon and carriage building practices of the time.

As mentioned previously, the works was self-reliant in terms of electricity production. The "Power House" was a major part of the plant: four steam-driven generators were provided-two each of 200 and 400Kw respectively. The generators were driven directly by Browett, Lindley triple-expansion vertical steam engines. Four Lancashire boil-

Dukinfield Carriage & Wagon Works, pre-WWI: This is a general view of the yard at the west end of the complex almost certainly taken from the 100,000 gallon water tank which was sited near the junction of Astley Street and Platt Street. The Power House, on Globe Lane, stands off to the right with its attendant chimney. Standing in front is a two-storey office building. Behind the siding roads can be seen the eight gables of the main shops; the chimney on the left would have served the boiler house and adjacent forge and smithy. Projecting just in front is the iron store, used in later years as an electrical assembly shop. Wagons of all shapes and sizes are lined up including one or two casualties awaiting their turn to go into the works for repair. On opposing sides of the picture can be seen quantities of wheels on axles all doubtless ready to be pressed into use. The white space on the right was dubbed "part of the reservoir" when this picture appeared in The Railway Magazine in 1914. The reservoir was, indeed, near here-but the actual ground that has been erased from the original photographic plate housed several chicken sheds and runs! Presumably the company did not want such mundane scenes to sully the pristine image of what was then a thoroughly up-to-date engineering concern. *National Railway Museum*

ers, each 30 ft.long by 8 ft. diameter provided steam. They were fed by mechanical stokers. All this, along with associated electrical equipment was housed in a building 145 ft.long and 60 ft.wide sited at the west end of the works, close by the mess room, just off Globe Lane. Steam from the engines was exhausted and then condensed by cooling water obtained from the nearby Peak Forest Canal owned, of course, by the GCR. Water from the canal was fed into reservoirs of 600,000 gallon capacity; these were sited at the west end of the works, between the canal and Astley Street. Further storage, of 100,000 gallons capacity, was maintained in tanks just by Platt Street and within the boundary of the complex. How long the self-sufficiency in electricity generation lasted is uncertain. However, a minute dated 27-12-1934 records that the supply of electricity to the works was by an "agreement with the Stalybridge, Hyde, Mossley and Dukinfield Tramways and Electricity Board."

Another important facility provided by the works was the air-compressing equipment housed near Dog Lane bridge (over the main line) at the west end of the works. This provided air at low pressure for the pneumatic signalling system installed on this stretch of the line. Other air compressors were housed in the power house for the various pneumatic tools in use within the plant. In here were installed hydraulic pumps which fed power for pressing carriage wheels onto axles. Via this arrangement also, carriage wheels could have their tyres removed without the need to remove the wheels from their axles.

All-in-all, the buildings at Dukinfield occupied about 12 acres of the total site area. As well as the Great Central's own rolling stock, Dukinfield handled the building and repair of vehicles for the CLC system and that of the MSJ&A. Few, if any, companies of the time had equipped themselves with such lavish and up-to-date accommodation for the maintenance and repair of their rolling stock as had the Great Central.

Some of the first vehicles to emerge from Dukinfield Works were the famous "Barnum" coaches. Alluding to American practice, these slab-sided coaches with their distinctive "matchboard" side panelling and railed end vestibules were a complete departure from anything seen hitherto on the GCR. Early products, too, from Dukinfield were the well-photographed "matchboard" coaches for main line use which were turned out in 1911. In contrast to the "Barnums" these had a conventional "tumblehome" to the sides. Contemporary with the "matchboard" main line stock were eight and ten compartment coaches (first and third class respectively) of 60 ft. length which were built for suburban working.

Though Dukinfield works managed to keep production of coaches and wagons going into the LNER era alarm bells were ringing there before the outbreak of the Second War. On December 15th.1938 a

Dukinfield Works, Interior, pre-WWI: A view looking down the Wagon Building Shop. Prominent on the left of the picture is a line of twelve 6-wheel 15 ton Brake Vans recorded as having been built here as part of a batch of 25 in 1911. Notice the staging projecting from the sides of the vans with crude wooden supports. This would be to enable construction to proceed on the upper parts of the vehicles. Crude-looking electric globes are suspended from the roof; one wonders what sort of light intensity such early fittings gave. In the centre can be seen rivetted steel underframes, possibly for more goods brakes. Notice the neat piles of timber all ready for assembly into more wagons and the completed goods vans over to the right. The neatness and orderliness of the shop show something of a contrast to the scenes inside Gorton Locomotive Works viewed earlier. *National Railway Museum*

question was put in Parliament by Mr.F.B.Simpson (the MP for Ashton-under-Lyne) to the Minister of Labour (Mr.Ernest Brown) asking him if he was was aware that the LNER were diverting coach-building away from Dukinfield. Mr.Brown went on to add that industry in his constituency was already depressed and pressed the minister on securing work for men who may be displaced.

The following June the LNER announced that carriage repair work hitherto carried out at Dukinfield would be distributed between Doncaster and York carriage shops. The forge and smithy at Dukinfield were to be retained and a proportion of the shops there would be utilised for the repair of wagons. Opportunity would be given for men to transfer to York as required. Later that month, in response to a question in Parliament, an announcement was made to the effect that about 200 men with "short service" at Dukinfield were to lose their jobs and a further 400 or so would be offered an opportunity of accepting work at York for wages of around 5/- to 10/- a week less.

In July it was confirmed by Captain Euan Wallace, then Minister of Transport, that no new wagon production would be undertaken at Dukinfield. The LNER had a surplus of wagons and new construction would concentrate on special types of vehicle.

Parliamentary acrimony developed further at the end of July when Mr.Wedgwood Benn, the MP for Gorton, joined the fray. Mr.Benn pressed Mr.Ernest Brown, Minister of Labour, on the question of government departments finding work for the men who had become displaced. A further Labour MP, Mr.Ellis Smith (the member for Stoke) raised the possibility of finding employment for the men in local industries engaged in aircraft production.

The remainder of the Dukinfield story is one of mixed fortunes. After the war the works was used for the scrapping of steam locomotives; there is a sad irony in seeing examples from former Great Central classes such as C4 (8B Atlantics), B1 (8C 4-6-0s) and B7 (9P 4-6-0s) dumped incongurously, stripped of cab and boiler mountings and waiting to be reduced to so much scrap.

But all was not lost: Metropolitan Vickers, electrical engineers, rented several bays in the works and fitted the electrical gear to the new Bo-Bo and Co-Co locomotives preparatory to the Manchester to Sheffield electrification. A map in the British Rail archives dated 1954 shows the western side of the works, the former carriage and wagon building and repair shops, designated as "Workshops/Stores and Loco assembly stores." BICC are also shown as tenants in the old Mess Room. Also built at Dukinfield were 60 001 Class (A) Co-Co Diesel Electric locomotives for the Irish railway system (CIE) between 1955-56. These were followed in 1956-57 by six Bo-Bo Diesel Electrics for the Northern Ireland system.

Another company, Robinson & Kershaw, used the east side of the works (the former carriage lifting and repair shop and timber drying shed) for fitting out engines built by Beyer, Peacock & Co. Robinson & Kershaw secured leases from the railway company; the first was dated December 30th.1947; a second lease, for 28 years, dated from June 24th.1948. Beyer,Peacock, of course, were a concern famous world-wide for their locomotive excellence and had rich historical links with the Great Central Railway. Sir Sam Fay became Chairman in 1923 and he was joined a year later by J.G.Robinson who took a Directorship there. Beyers had been contracted to build the famous "Hymek" Diesels which took to the rails in 1961; these also had equipment fitted at Dukinfield, including the brakegear-a product of Davies & Metcalfe in Romiley, Stockport.

Wagon building appears to have ceased at Dukinfield after the war; it is known, though, that wagon repairs were being done there concurrent with the work on the electric locomotives in the early 1950s. British Railways relinquished responsibility for the site in 1962. Looking at Dukinfield Works today, for the bulk of the plant is still standing, is to gaze on the optimism and confidence of a great Edwardian enterprise, one which was fuelled by the spirit and beliefs of men in an age, far removed from our own, when the railway had no serious rival in the field of inland transport. In the palmy days of Edwardian Britain, such men could not have foreseen the disaster that was the First World War, the disappearance of their organisation that was precipitated by it, the depression that followed and the enforced rationalisation that preceeded yet another war. Dukinfield Carriage and Wagon Works, a child of its time, has passed into history.

Dukinfield Carriage & Wagon Works, November 3rd.1948. A sad and melancholy sight and a reminder of the diverse nature of work undertaken at Dukinfield since the late 1930s. Former Great Central Atlantic No.**2915** stands in a line of compatriots outside the main works building awaiting its call to the cutter's torch. Formerly No.1092 of GCR Class 8B (LNER C4), the engine was one of a batch of 12 Simple Atlantics built by the North British Locomotive Company in October and November 1905. Withdrawn from traffic the previous month, No.2915 is one of several ex-GCR engines which were stored here prior to cutting up. Other known former GCR examples stored at Dukinfield (but not necessarily cut up there) were B4 No.1486; B6 Nos.1346 & 1347; B7 Nos.61707 & 61712 (these BR numbers being the second post-LNER numbers in both cases). B8 No.1349; B9 Nos.1471, 1478 & 61475; B18 No.1480; C4 Nos.2903, 2917 & 2924; C5 No.2897; F2 Tank No.7104. Notice the camouflage markings on the outside wall; part of the works had re-opened in the Second World War for shell production. *R.E. Gee.*

Dewsnap Sidings, May 9th.1953: B1 No.**61174** clears the end of the siding complex and heads along the Up Fast line towards Hyde Junction. A glimpse of activity inside the former Dukinfield Carriage and Wagon Works can be seen behind the iron railings on the left-hand side. The photographer is standing by the Down Goods No.2 Loop which extended as far as Hyde Junction. The piles of spoil just behind the locomotive are colliery waste dumped from the former mines which existed here to the north-east side of the yard.

B.K.B.Green

Between Dewsnap and Hyde Junction, April 12th.1954: No.69999 has left Dewsnap on its Spring outing and is edging along the Up Through Siding towards Hyde Junction. Hyde Junction had a complicated track layout brought about by the widening in the early years of the century. The photograph reveals something of this: main lines to the left, goods lines to the right with crossovers between the two pairs of roads. From just where the photographer is standing another set of switches allows traffic on the Up and Down main lines to run either along the Joint line via Woodley or across on to the ex-GCR line towards Godley. Notice the Down Goods No.2 road forks away to the left just by the overbridge ahead-where our picture featuring the wiring train is located. The Garratt is passing the works of Daniel Adamson & Co. (of Manchester Ship Canal fame). The gantry seen in the picture belonged to an overhead crane which was used for loading and off-loading goods in the company's yard to and from the railway. Adamson's works locomotive was quite well-known in this locality and was named "Little Enoch." The sidings at Adamson's works were taken out of use on November 19th.1967. *B.K.B.Green*

Hyde Junction, early 1950s: A group of overhead line engineers and their wiring train take possession of the Down main line at Hyde Junction whilst the finishing touches are put to the overhead catenary. The coaches, former Great Eastern stock, have a specially-constructed flat section, to enable the crew to walk the length of the train without hindrance. Of interest is the attire of the personnel: Duffle coats seem to have been de rigeur for senior technicians in those days. Hard hats and yellow vests had yet to come on the scene. Spanning the tracks here is the Wood Street footbridge (bridge 32) connecting Wood Street and Railway Street, across to the left of the picture, with Dewsnap Lane-just visible on the right. A railway from Victoria Colliery - on the north side of the line - once crossed the Woodhead line via bridge 32. Notice the entrance to the Down goods loop, on the bottom left-hand side, extending from here to Guide Bridge. *W.S.Garth*

Hyde Junction was the focal point of the Midland Railway's first incursion into the North-West in order to reach Manchester and, eventually, Merseyside. It was to Hyde (later Hyde Central) that the MS&L had opened a branch in March 1858. Later that year an extension to Marple was proposed in the form of the Marple, New Mills and Hayfield Junction Railway. On July 1st.1865 the Midland arrived from Millers Dale to meet the MS&L at New Mills. Thus was formed in 1868 one of the most important alliances in North-West railway history: the Sheffield and Midland Joint Committee: later to beçome the Great Central & Midland Joint. So over this section of line via Romiley and Woodley the Midland Railway would have run its London to Manchester Expresses-initially from King's Cross-hauled by pretty little Kirtley 2-2-2 green engines drawing trains of 6-wheeled coaches painted in the beautiful crimson lake that was so much the company's hallmark. What a splendid contrast all this must have made at Hyde Junction with the MS&L's trains adorned in varnished Teak and drawn by elegant-looking Sacré 2-4-0s and 4-4-0s bedecked in a different shade of green.

Hyde Junction, May 9th.1953: Pre-Grouping glories and liveries are but a distant memory at Hyde Junction now. The "overhead" is in place and,soon, the sights and sounds of the steam locomotive will have gone. Class 04/7 No.**63843** slogs along the Up Through Siding from the direction of Dewsnap Sidings and is ascending the 1-in-97 towards the station with an east-bound (Up) Class H (mixed) freight train. The former Sheffield and Midland joint line from Woodley via Apethorne Junction cuts in from the left and joins the ex-GCR main line at this point to become Up and Down Main respectively. Past the photographer, lever No.6 will have been pulled out and the 04 will cross over to the right to join the Up Main towards Godley Junction. Notice that colour lights are in position to replace the historic electro-pneumatic semaphores once such a feature of this section of the Woodhead route. *B.K.B.Green*

Hyde Junction, c.1930s: Class D11 "Director" 4-4-0 No.**5511** *Marne* passes the signalbox and heads along the Up Main line with an express. From this point she will swing over the junction and gain the GCR main line towards Godley. *GCRS Collection*

Hyde Junction, c.1948: A five-coach stopping train composed entirely of ex-GCR stock passes along the main line drawn by C14 Tank No.**67449**. To the side of the line can be seen the engineering works of Daniel Adamson & Co. It was Adamson who was the pioneering force behind the building of the Manchester Ship Canal stemming from a meeting held at his house in Didsbury, South Manchester in June 1882. Returning our gaze to the station we can see that a Manchester-bound train has just left from the Down platform having deposited a small cluster of passengers who can be seen walking towards the station exit past the booking office. Leading the way is an oldish man, cigarette in mouth, cloth cap on head and carrying s small suitcase. Behind comes a smartly-dressed lady, complete with hat and suit, clasping the hand of an elder-possibly her mother, a little girl jogs along just in front. A typical family group, maybe returning via the Joint line from an outing in Derbyshire or perhaps an elderly couple being met off the train by their daughter and grand-daughter. Such scenes tell us much about the changes in travel over the last forty-odd years or so. Today, the all-pervading car would be used for such trips; and though it possible, still, to reach New Mills from Hyde; rail travel to beauty spots south of Chinley-such as Millers Dale, Monsal Dale, Darley Dale and Matlock is, regrettably, no longer possible. Hyde Junction station changed its name to Hyde North on September 17th.1951. *W.A.Camwell*

Hyde North, 1957: The fine buildings at Hyde North ("Hyde Junction" prior to September 17th 1951). This is the Down platform on the Joint line via Woodley. It was via this line that Midland Railway trains first gained access to Manchester London Road. Our picture was taken just prior to demolition of the quite splendid buildings which were very similar in style to those at neighbouring Hyde Central. MS&L influence is apparent and similar features were to be seen at Hazlehead. A new station, Flowery Field, for passengers travelling on Manchester to Glossop and Hadfield services, was opened in 1985 to provide a more convenient access to the Bennett Street area than the somewhat lonely footpath serving Hyde North. Flowery Field, situated a quarter of a mile or so up the line towards Newton, was opened officially in August 1985 at areported cost of £100,00. ***Reporter Group of Newspapers***

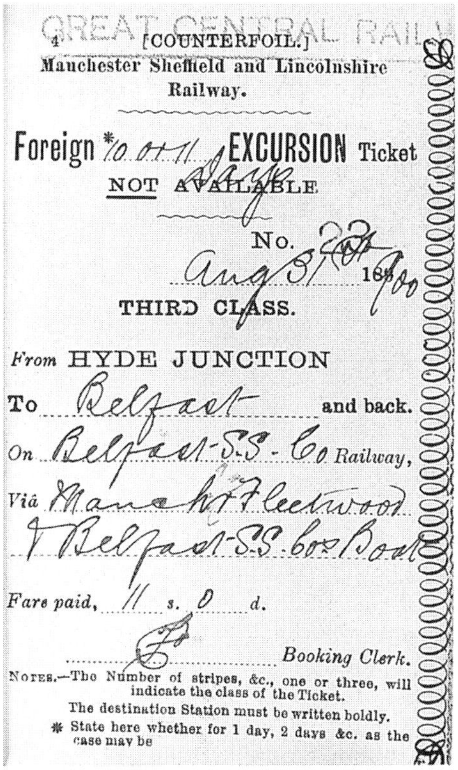

GREAT CENTRAL RAIL

4 [COUNTERFOIL.]

Manchester Sheffield and Lincolnshire Railway.

Foreign *10 or 11 days EXCURSION Ticket

NOT AVAILABLE

No. 23

Aug 31st 1900

THIRD CLASS.

From HYDE JUNCTION

To Belfast and back.

On Belfast S.S. Co Railway,

Viâ Manchr Fleetwood & Belfast S.S. Co's Boat

Fare paid, 11 s. 0 d.

Booking Clerk.

NOTES.—The Number of stripes, &c., one or three, will indicate the class of the Ticket.

The destination Station must be written boldly.

* State here whether for 1 day, 2 days &c. as the case may be

Bargain travel from Hyde Junction: A counterfoil of an excursion ticket issued from here on August 31st.1900 for a 10 or 11 day foreign (sic) excursion to Belfast and back. Note the appearance of the MS&L's title on the ticket top and the over-stamping of "Great Central Railway".

Clearing Hyde Junction and leaving the Sheffield and Midland Joint line curving away to the right, the rising gradient eases slightly towards milepost 7 from 1-in-97 to 1-in-185. Shaking off the conurbations of east Manchester and the fringes of Ashton-under-Lyne and Stockport, the Woodhead line is now heading towards open country.

"Newton for Hyde" is sited 2¼ miles from Guide Bridge and 7¼ miles from Manchester. Opened in 1841 with the first section of line, the earliest station at Newton would have been a single-platform affair with a building little more than a shed.

Newton for Hyde, July 1971: A Class 506 EMU with Driving Trailer Second No.**M59605M** leading stands in the station with an afternoon service en route to Hadfield. The simple stone structure of the Down platform building with elegant curved stone lintels over the windows make for interesting architectural details. A sign on the left-hand side, by the fence, directs passengers towards the subway-bridge No.38A constructed in 1893 and linking the Up and Down platforms.

W.A.Brown

East of Newton, April 15th.1954: B1 No.**61150** charges along up the 1-in-143 gradient beyind Newton station at the head of a 9-coach express. The buildings in the background belong to the Harbour Farm estate. Today, the M67 motorway has irretrievably altered the landscape here-making an artificial valley over which the railway is carried on a rather unspectacular deck of concrete.

B.K.B.Green

Between Newton and Godley, April 15th.1954: Though such matters will always be the subject of argument, Gresley's Pacifics were, for many enthusiats, the British railway express steam locomotive par excellence. Power and majesty seem to ooze from A3 No.**60059** *Tracery* as she clears Highfield bridge and storms along towards Godley with a 10-coach express. The "overhead" is up and ready to go; on the right-hand side of the track can be seen the 33,000 volt feeder cables which will supply three phase alternating current to the various substations along the route. *B.K.B.Green*

Between Newton and Godley, April 15th.1954: Barm House bridge (numbered 41) was one of the earliest structures on this section of line to have survived in its entirety with minimal alteration. This splendid example of the civil engineer's art consisted of three elliptical brick arches and dated from 1840. The bridge carried Barm House Road and linked the appropriately-named Sheffield Road with open land that fringed on to Godley reservoir. In what would be the last months of steam here, motor-fitted C14 No.**67417** clatters beneath the bridge en route to Glossop with a two coach push-pull working. *B.K.B.Green*

Between Newton and Godley, June 4th 1954: Just to prove that Gresley's engines didn't dominate on all the workings over Woodhead. Here is a B16/3-No **61464**-a Raven design dating initially from 1919 for the North Eastern Railway, but rebuilt by Edward Thompson in 1944 with Walschaerts valve gear. The Up through goods train has just passed under Barm House bridge and the train is now veering towards more open terrain. Notice the air main alongside the Down line; Newton was the last outpost of the former GCR's pneumatic signalling system. ***B.K.B.Green***

Godley Junction Station, n.d: Evoking memories of Pre-Grouping traffic through here is *Glenalmond* (GCR Class 1A) 4-6-0 No.**442** about to enter the station with an Up express freight train. Liveried in plain black, lined red and white, these mixed-traffic locomotives were a 5'-4"-wheeled version of J.G.Robinson's handsome, but somewhat mediocre, "Sir Sam Fay" express engine of 1912. *Author's collection*

The name "Godley" featured early on in the annals of the first railway between Manchester and Sheffield. It was to this place, then no more than a village on the old Sheffield road, that the initial section of railway from Manchester to Sheffield opened far back in November, 1841. This first station at Godley, a temporary affair which lasted little more than a year, was sited close to the Hyde and Mottram Road (now the A57). The term "Godley Toll Bar"mentioned in early literature indicates the status of the road at that time. Godley acquired a permanent station some twenty-four years later when, on February 1st.1866, a junction with the MS&L line was established and the railway from here south-west to Woodley, via Apethorne Junction, was opened for traffic.

Godley Junction station, named plain "Godley" thus needed four platform faces and served two masters-the CLC, of which the MS&L was of course a member, and the parent company itself. The link to Woodley and thence Stockport and westwards to Liverpool was of momentous importance to the MS&L, giving direct access to the port of Liverpool without the need to go via Manchester. Thus, travelling westwards, Godley became the point where freight traffic from as far afield as Merseyside interfaced with that going to and fro over the Pennines. Intechange sidings became a necessary requirement for the breaking-up and change-over of freight traffic and two main siding sets were provided: those adjacent to the CLC line, known as Brookfold Sidings and those lying alongside the Up Sheffield line under the control of the eastern company.

In the era of electrification Godley became the point where steam, and later Diesel, gave way to electric traction and vice versa for traffic emanating over the former CLC system and continuing over the Pennines via Woodhead. A traction change-over siding was sited here and two loops, one on either side of the line, ran between Godley Junction and a point some 700 yards east. This point of entry and exit was controlled by its own signalbox known as "Godley East".

When the loops were being lengthened in 1915, doubtless to aid the passage of coal traffic for the war effort, a serious landslip occured in the deep cutting entombing two workmen. At Godley East the loops joined the main line and the double track formation continued as far as Mottram No.1 signalbox-where the entrance to Mottram yard was sited, a little east ofmilepost 10¼.

Brookfold boasted its own signalbox and turntable. A CLC traffic control office was based at Godley as was one of the LNER's wartime operational headquarters. Controlling operations as far east as Wath and Doncaster, the building was deemed to be bomb proof. Equipped with parquet flooring and cast iron stoves, it was sited in a single-storey building alongside the rear of the Up main line platform.

Godley Junction, n.d: Godley in the pre-Group area. The canopies on the Down island platform, covered footbridge and roofed waiting shelter on the GC Up platform had all been swept away by the 1950s. The tall lattice-post signals were a distinctive CLC feature and would have dated from the inauguration of the CLC line to Apethorne in 1866. The ash-ballasted trackwork and the presence of 6-wheeled passenger stock in the goods yard all point to a view well before the turn of the century. Notice the junction signalbox has yet to occupy its later position at the end of the Up GCR platform. *Collection of J.Ryan/J.A.Peden*

Godley Junction, April 22nd.1976: A series of three photographs showing a sequence of movements at Godley involving through workings to and from the CLC line and the resultant traction change-over pattern. (Top) A train load of empty MGR hopper wagons has arrived at Brookfold Sidings and are waiting in the Up Loop in front of the signal box. Electric traction in the form of Nos.**76008** and **76006** cross over from the Down to Up line to take their charge eastwards over the Pennines.
(*bottom*) The engines have backed from the Up CLC line into the Up Loop. The "doll" is off and the ensemble is drawing forward towards Brookfold signal box. Coming slowly along the Down Through Siding is Class 40 No.**113** on a coke train. This siding was an extension of the Down Goods line which had begun further back along the GC main line at Godley East. The modern-looking building in the background is the purpose-built factory of Messrs.Walls and was geared entirely towards the production of Pork and Bacon products. The company were a major employer in the Godley area at this time.
(*opposite-bottom*) The two Bo-Bos await the "right away" before proceeding across the junction to join the Up main line. On the Down line a train of bogie bolster wagons loaded with steel is awaiting departure down to Apethorne Junction. Re-ballasting has taken place here of late and notice the abandoned turntable pit (taken out of use on April 1st.1969) in the foreground-just visible through the early Spring foliage. The monstrous-looking skyscraper flats of Hattersley make for an ugly blot on the horizon.

Raymond Keeley

Godley Junction, August 11th 1978: Latter days of freight traffic on the Woodhead line. Bo-Bo No **76051** (ex EM 1 No 26051 *Mentor*) approaches Godley Junction from the east with a Down coal working. The empty sidings, referred to elsewhere in the text, in the right foreground sprout a mass of overgrowth and give some indication of the run-down of traffic on this route. High-rise flats dominate the background; the area round here and neighbouring Hattersley having been colonised by Manchester City council since the early 1960s for a substantial overspill estate complete with its own railway station. ***W.A.Brown***

Godley Junction station, April 10th.1954: Viewed from the footbridge, O4/3 No.**63742** heads east through the station with a through loose-coupled freight train of mixed proportions. The two-storey building in the right background was the MS&L signal and telegraph store, a use continued by the building until modern times. Next to it is the former wartime headquarters of the LNER referred to earlier. Notice the shutters still hanging adjacent to the windows-the war had ended only a bare nine years previously! Of interest are the "Naval Store" tanker wagons in the goods yard and the prevalence of so many wooden bodied coal wagons in the sidings. The winding lane to the left is Station Road; a cluster of attractive houses, former dwellings owned by the railway company, still stand at the top here, behind the photographer. *B.K.B.Green*

Godley Junction, n.d: A somewhat battered, but nevertheless very interesting, pre-War view of the Godley junction "Pilot". N5 0-6-2 tank No.**5912** (BR 69336) is standing between duties in the CLC yard; the Down platform can be seen behind. Despite being an everyday part of the railway scene, activity like this has rarely been recorded for posterity. Seen around the engine are Mac Clist, (?)Lack, Jimmy Wilcox, C.Humphreys, T.Gardner, Jack Hurst, Alf Reimer (a Foreman), Mick Robinson (Driver) and Arnold Wilson (Fireman). *Collection of A.M.West.*

Godley Junction, August 1965: Clear blue skies herald a fine summer day at Godley, an occasion that was something of a red-letter day for young Andrew West who appeared to have been given the "freedom of the city" here just for the day. Andrew, a correspondent from Ipswich, Australia, was taken by Jimmy Wilcox, a shunter at Godley and treated, amongst other things, to a visit to the signalbox and various footplates rides. Here he is, under Jimmy's supervision, on the footplate of green-liveried Class EM1 Bo-Bo No.**26048** *Hector*. The engine is standing at the end of the Up CLC platform. Of interest is the grounded 6-wheeled coach body on the platform, no doubt serving as Mess quarters and the water tank in the background. *Collection of A.M.West*

Godley Junction, mid-1950s: A view from the cab of a speeding electric engine en route through here on the Down main line. This panoramic view gives an excellent impression of the layout at Godley and makes for an amazing contrast with the earlier nineteenth century study. The CLC line down to Apethorne sweeps off to the left; the yard behind is well stocked with vehicles. In front of the box vans Mess cabins stand where some degree of shelter and comfort was provided for men like Jimmy Wilcox, Jack Hurst and Alf Reimer who must have spent a lifetime here-unsung heroes keeping the traffic moving 24 hours a day in all weathers. The Down Goods line (which commenced at Godley East) parallels the main line and continues as the Down Through Siding to the left of the island platform. Passenger trains were allowed to use this track in an emergency with the proviso that their speed was not to exceed 10 miles per hour. Fanning out in front of the Mess cabins can be seen four siding roads. these each had a recorded capacity of (l to r) 49, 34, 31 and 31 wagons respectively. Beyond the CLC line platforms, in Brookfold Sidings, an electric engine has emerged from the Up Loop and is waiting for the road across the junction after the signalman has given "train out of section" for our express. Over on the right, in the former GC yard, another "juice engine" awaits its next turn of duty. The Up Goods loop, from Godley East, fed into this yard. Six sidings were provided here latterly with a recorded capacity of 162 wagons. *B.K.B.Green*

Godley Junction, September 7th.1971: A view looking east to Mottram from the end of the island platform. The T-shirted signalman glances out from the end of the substantial-looking GCsignal box as a Class 506 3-Car EMU set (Motor Open Brake Second **M59405M** leading) approaches forming a Down stopping train en route for Manchester Piccadilly. The small building in front of the signalbox was a Mess cabin, one of several in the immediate vicinity which provided shelter for the numerous shunters, tappers, foremen, guards and enginemen who were deployed in what was once a welter of activity at this, a very busy and key location. Over on the CLC side, a Class 40 Diesel bearing the headcode AL 75 and at the head of a loaded MGR train waits for the road out of the yard and along the Through Siding before heading down the former CLC line in the direction of Apethorne Junction. *W.A.Brown*

Godley East Junction, May 1952: B1 No.**61160** passes the junction with a Down Express. Loops on either side of the line ran for almost half a mile from here to Godley Junction. A serious landslip occured here on Friday March 13th.1915 when the loops were being lengthened. About 40 men were engaged, a number of whom were seated on the opposite side of the line having just finished their midday meal. Suddenly, a mass of earth was seen to move. A warning was shouted to the men who were seated, most of whom managed to run clear. Unfortunately two did not escape and were entombed in a mass of soil and stone which broke away from the cutting and spread itself over the permanent way, blocking it for several hours. Some idea of the extent of the slip can be gauged from the fact that the soil covered the line for a distance of about 50 yards to a depth of 3 feet. The width of the cavity in the cutting caused by the fall of earth was about 20 yards. Notice the lattice post signal, colour lights were still two years away, and the catch points at the end of the Down loop designed to protect the main line from errant vehicles on the 1-in-143 gradient. *J.Davenport*

Godley East Junction,c.Summer 1954: A splenid study of steam, smoke sunlight and shade as O4/1 No.**63614** slogs up the 1-in-143 towards Mottram with a west-bound Class B freight train. The engine is passing the approximate point of the west portal of the former Hattersley tunnel No.1. In the rebuilding programme the track formation was raised slightly and a new drainage system was installed. Notice the void on the left-hand side of the permanent way. This would have been left behind when the temporary trackwork put in to carry the traffic to the south of the tunnels was removed. On the right can be seen part of the retaining wall installed to keep earth movement at bay during the excavations. In the 1915 works the Godley loops were lengthened from 18 chains to 24¼ chains (18¾ - 24). Godley East was re-positioned approximately 24 chains east - presumably at the same time. *Tom Lewis*

Looking to Godley East Junction, later 1950s: An aerial view at Godley East and one providing a distinct contrast to pictures seen just previously. After about 110 years steam has now vanished from the Woodhead line making this Britian's first "all-electric" main line railway. Co-Co Electric No.**27004** *Juno* heads through the massive cutting with an Up express. This picture shows the rough extent of the two former Hattersley tunnels. No.1 tunnel had its western-most portal just near to Godley East Junction box-feintly visible far left. This first tunnel, 55 yards in length was separated from the second tunnel by an open space 154 yards long. This photograph was taken from the A560 Glossop to Stockport road bridge, built approximately mid-way over the second tunnel.

It was in the open space between the tunnels, on Saturday February 7th.1920, that a serious collision occured. Due to heavy snow falls and high winds all the block wires between Mottram and Godley East were down and emergency working to Rule 25 under "caution" was in force with a 10 minute interval being allowed between successive trains.

At 8.59 a goods train standing at the Godley East Home signal was run into by a passenger train consisting of eight carriages, weight 181 tons and drawn by a 4-4-2 tank engine. No.2 tunnel was thick with smoke, an Up train having just run through, and the driver's visibility was thus seriously impaired. Driver Morton, in charge of the passenger train, estimated that his speed was between 10 and 15 miles an hour when the impact occured. Considerable damage was done to the goods train; the guard sustaining serious injuries as a result and having to be conveyed by train to Manchester's Royal Infirmary.

At the Inquiry, Colonel Pringle criticised signalman Martin (at Mottram) for not having stopped the passenger train in order to pass the verbal "caution" to both the driver and the guard. The Inspector was also critical of the railway company's failure to consider some kind of emergency "field" telephone system between signalboxes in times of block failures. 56 hours had elapsed at Godley during which time "caution" working had been in force. Morton had travelled two or three times over the route in that time, but was not, nevertheless, exercising proper caution, the Colonel said. He was also critical of the lack of any emergency first-aid dressings in the brake van of the passenger train and stated that the injured should not have had to await the arrival of the breakdown crane or the emergency services before their wounds could be tended.

Tom Lewis

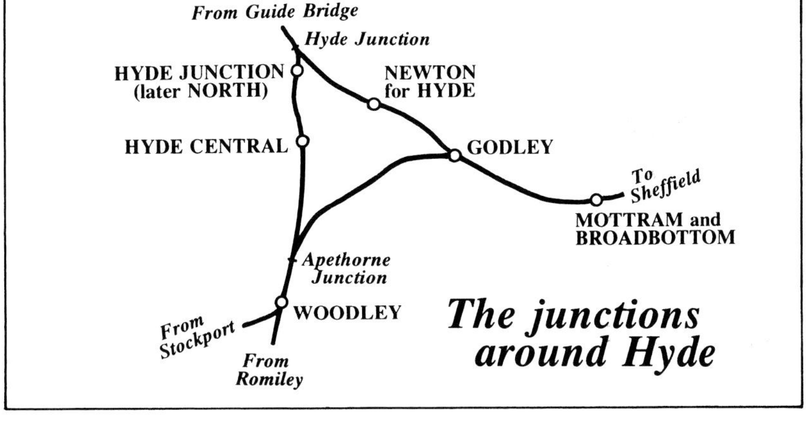

In December 1926 Charles.C.Brown, the LNER's Chief Civil Engineer reported to the Board on the deteriorating situation of the tunnel linings. After considering the available options-rebuilding or repairing the tunnels, only one feasible alternative was left: the two Hattersley tunnels would have to be removed.

In November 1927 the decision was announced that work to open out the tunnels was to commence almost forthwith. Such a move cannot have been made lightly. The LNER contract drawings, dated November 14th.1927, reveal the tunnel linings to be around 3'-0" thick at their base. Aside from the removal of this formidable mass of brickwork, the former GCR main line was then literally teeming with freight, especially coal, traffic and it was clear that some extraordinary contingencies would be needed to sustain the flow of that traffic while the work of opening out the massive brick-lined structures was undertaken. The official reasons advanced for the tunnels' removal were the increased dimensions of the, then, present-day rolling stock and the requirement for four tracks on a busy section of the line. 700,000 cubic yards of earth were removed in this operation, the contract for which was awarded to Messrs.Logan and Hemmingway.

Work began early in 1928 and was completed in 1931. The vast amount of spoil removed was deposited in the area known as Great Wood, near Broadbottom. To facilitate movement of the contractor's vehicles and plant whilst the tunnels were removed, a length of standard gauge railway was laid alongside the tunnels on either side of the line. In addition to this, a temporary crossover was laid to the east of the second tunnel and a further temporary line trailed off the Down main into Great Wood to enable the direct tipping of spoil.

Once sufficient spoil had been removed, and only the tunnel brickwork remained with a minimum top covering, a temporary deviation had to be inserted in the main line in order to keep the traffic moving while the demolition work was completed. This left the existing line on the Down side at a point east of the second tunnel, rose on a gradient of 1-in-133/1-in-176 through the cutting behind the tunnels and then fell at 1-in 125/1-in-73 to re-join the main line just west of Godley East Junction signalbox. The immensity of the work can be gleaned from the photographs. Logan and Hemmingway faced almost insuperable difficulties, having come across unexpectedly large amounts of water in their excavations. The LNER did allow the company an extra sum of £13,339. A request, however, that an extra 6d per cubic yard for soil excavated (an increase over the original 1/6d per cu.yd. quoted) was turned down. Such were the difficulties facing contractors in Britain over 60 years ago.

The Glossop to Stockport Road (Mottram Old Road-once a Roman Road, then the A560) passed more or less over the centre of the second (eastern-most) tunnel). Prior to the opening-out operation the road was diveretd to the west. In consequence an impressive viaduct was constructed. Listed as bridge No.46 this consisted of 5 spans, 40 feet between the parapets with a height of 52'-6" above rail-level. Records show the bridge as having been constructed in 1925. Though this was some time before the decision to open the tunnels out had been announced, some forward planning must have been in the offing to warrant such a substantial work. An interesting sidelight is thrown on the work by the fact that, although the bridge was maintained by the railway company, (LNER and later BTC), it was constructed and owned by the Ministry of Transport. Maintenance was "at cost of ministry." A serious slip in the cutting in later years resulted in some major reconstruction work. (Q.V.)

Hattersley Tunnels, c.1928: A view looking west towards Godley from the Glossop Road bridge. The eastern portal of No.1 tunnel displays the dark entrance to its confines during the last weeks of its existence. Something of the scale of the mammoth undertaking can be gleaned here: the mound in the bottom right of our picture disguises the remnants of No.2 tunnel, the longer of the two bores. To the left of the crane, which stands alongside the tunnel entrance, the formation of the temporary Up line takes shape at a marginally higher level than the main line. Appearing little more than ants, workmen in their dozens are spread over the scene. The overall view illustrates well traditional railway design and construction methods with earthworks on a very grand scale having been thought necessary. Extensive drainage designed to aid an efficient dispersal of water from the slopes-witness the profusion of channels appearing in the cutting sides. As mentioned in the introduction, the design certainly suggests the possibility of allowing for a formation of four tracks; though, of course, this was never realised. In the event, the sections of railway trackbed, formerly in the tunnel, were protected from invasion by any spoil from the newly-created cutting by retaining walls, features which are still extant today.

Edward Wrathall

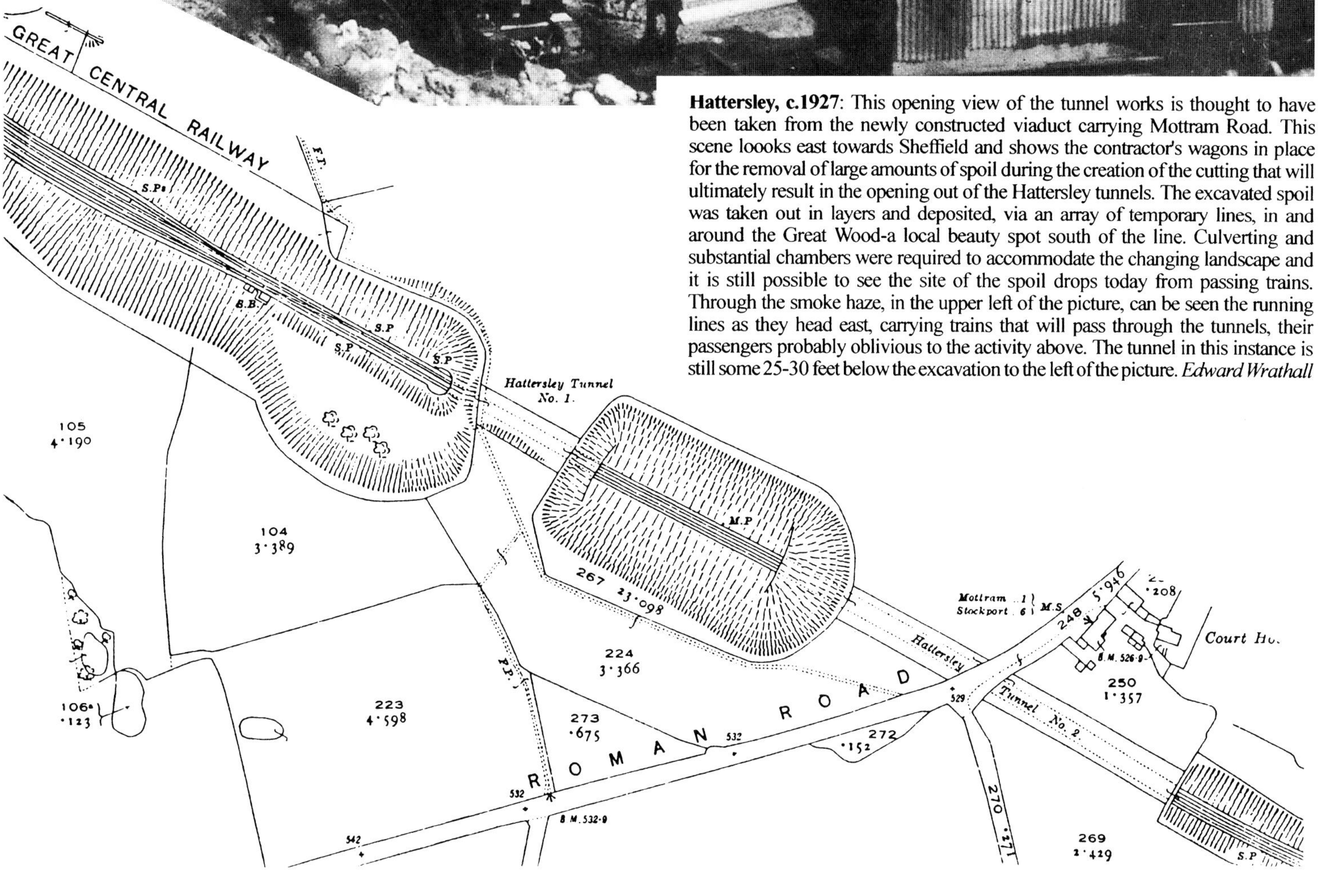

Hattersley, c.1927: This opening view of the tunnel works is thought to have been taken from the newly constructed viaduct carrying Mottram Road. This scene loooks east towards Sheffield and shows the contractor's wagons in place for the removal of large amounts of spoil during the creation of the cutting that will ultimately result in the opening out of the Hattersley tunnels. The excavated spoil was taken out in layers and deposited, via an array of temporary lines, in and around the Great Wood-a local beauty spot south of the line. Culverting and substantial chambers were required to accommodate the changing landscape and it is still possible to see the site of the spoil drops today from passing trains. Through the smoke haze, in the upper left of the picture, can be seen the running lines as they head east, carrying trains that will pass through the tunnels, their passengers probably oblivious to the activity above. The tunnel in this instance is still some 25-30 feet below the excavation to the left of the picture. *Edward Wrathall*

Godley East Junction, n.d: A view looking east through the tunnels from rail-level. Materials litter the lineside and the excavation work is almost complete. A "C" sign is in position to warn drivers of work ahead: the surrounding spoil over both tunnels has all but been removed; a ten-foot thickness remains to provide stability whilst traffic continues. Now the contractors have an awesome task-the removal of over 300 yards of arched brickwork and topsoil. Notice the wooden "gallows" signal gantry spanning both tracks. This carries two lower quadrant home signals for Godley East Junction box-seen off to the right: one signal is for the Down Main, the other for the Down Loop. Work is in hand behind the signalbox on the earthworks required to carry the temporary Down line. Upon completion of this link, capacity of the tunnel would be reduced to a single line for Up trains only. Faintly discernible in the background is the outline of the new Hattersley viaduct. Hattersley station-opened in May 1978, is sited approximately where the two loops begin. ***Edward Wrathall***

Hattersley No.1 Tunnel c.1928: A rare view of the No.1, the western-most of the two Hattersley tunnels, taken from the side of the cutting before excavation work had begun. An LNER Class B3(GCR Class 9P) 4-6-0 is about to enter the tunnel in full cry with an Up express. White heat is seen at the firehole door, a copious mane of exhaust billows back from the chimney and the safety valves of the fine-looking engine are lifting. On the skyline a steam-powered excavator is seen at work. This may have been engaged in preparatory work on the tunnel removal or during work on the Glossop Road deviation which produced the magnificent viaduct seen and mentioned elsewhere. *Edward Wrathall*

Godley East Junction, n.d: This was the view looking west from Godley East Junction signalbox. Passing the end of the two loops is an ex-Great Central "Sir Sam Fay" 4-6-0 (now LNER Class B1) at the head of a 5-coach Up express. A tall lower-quadrant signal guards the exit from the Up loop while, on the Down Main, the Starter is pegged "off" for yet another train. A once everyday scene taken for granted at the time and now part of the history of a once great railway line. *Edward Wrathall*

Hattersley Tunnel Approach, n.d: A fine period view exemplifying express working over the Woodhead route in the pre-WW1 period. Great Central Atlantic No.**1094**. The train, a Down express would appear to have just cleared Hattersley Tunnel No.1 and would be approaching Godley Junction. The coaching stock is in the two-tone brown with cream upper panels introduced towards the end of 1903. The appearance of the carriages bears a striking resemblance to that of contemporary Great Western practice; though the Great Central abandoned the clerestory roof in 1905. No.1094 was the last of a batch of twelve of J.G.Robinson's celebrated Atlantics built for the GCR by the North British Loco.Company in 1905.
F.E.Mackey/Collection of W.A.Brown

Hattersley Viaduct, Bridge No.46. December 1st.1960: A view from track-level showing the alarming drop on the south side of the structure due to the cutting slip and consequent settling of the brick pier. Close scrutiny of the original picture shows an upward movement of the cutting soil caused by the downward pressure of many hundreds of tons of brick and steel. Freedom from trains for a few minutes or so gives a chance to examine the design of the catenary supports. The cross-bracing with an "I" section girder was required for the heavier section of wire and associated catenary needed for the 1500V Dc system. When this picture was taken the Manchester-Crewe 25kV Ac electrification was well complete and pointed the way to the future. Would such a system have saved Woodhead? *British Railways*

Hattersley Viaduct, Bridge No.46. May 19th.1961: A close up of the viaduct showing the extent of the collapse and the supporting methods being put into place prior to the building of a new brick pier. Looking upwards from the railway we observe something of the old Hattersley before much of the present-day estate sprang up. The name "Hattersley" is derived from Addersley meaning a field of adders. Margaret Knott, a local historian, remembers Hattersley as: "*a green and pleasant oasis, where cattle and poultry roamed freely on farmland. It was a place where wild flowers and crops grew in meadows and fields smelled sweetly of fresh cut hay. Children and their bikes would free-wheel down the lanes.*" This photograph and Margaret's fond reminiscencies make for a stark contrast with the Hattersley of today. *British Railways*

East of Godley, A560 road bridge-April 10th.1954: A panoramic view of O4/3 No.**63742** at the head of an Up freight train gives us the opportunity to divert our eyes from track level and look upwards at the massive 5-span structure spanning the railway between Godley and Mottram. Referred to in official records as bridge No.46, the structure was known locally as "Hattersley Viaduct." In the latter part of 1960 a slip in the cutting slope caused one of the brick piers on the south side of the bridge to settle. This caused an alarming tilt at one end of the structure and the road had to be closed for some twelve months whilst the damage was repaired.
B.K.B.Green

Between Godley East Junction and Mottram c.Spring 1954: "All systems go" looks likely for the "overhead" as K3 No.**61852** clears the viaduct and heads towards Mottram with an Up express working. Descending the 1-in-143, a goods train makes a no doubt cautious passage towards the loops at Godley East. 61852, then a Gorton engine, was transferred to Lincoln in June 1954. It ended its days at Colwick and was cut up at Doncaster in July, 1961. *Tom Lewis*

Officialdom has never seemed quite certain what to call the station lying at OS grid reference 63 SJ 99 and situated between milepost $9\frac{3}{4}$ and 10. The Sheffield, Ashton-under-Lyne & Manchester Railway called it "Broadbottom" when it opened for passengers on December 10th 1842. Less than three years later, in July 1845, it became "Mottram". Undecided that this name was appropriate the MS&L decided on the best of both worlds when they renamed the station "Mottram and Broadbottom" as and from May 1st.1884. Modern officials were, seemingly, not happy with such duplicity and the station reverted to its original title from January 1st.1954. Something of the former legend, though, was applied with the suffix "for Mottram and Charlesworth" remaining in use until comparatively recently. Goods facilities here ceased on July 15th.1963 and the station remains open today. Catering for never more than local traffic the station did have a moment of glory in the 1920s when, for a short period, the morning restaurant car express from Manchester to Marylebone called here.

Broadbottom (for Mottram and Charlesworth), July 1971: Entering the station from Mottram Road this was the entrance as seen by passengers over no less than one and a quarter centuries. Splendid, yet discretely shabby, there is something quite magnificent here at Broadbottom. Doubtless the late Sir John Betjeman would have eulogised at the site of such elegance. Under the heading "bus services" it is announced that local Area Manager Mr.B.K.Shaw will be pleased to help you if you have a travel problem. In recent times a fire caused substantial damage at Broadbottom station. Happily, the station was rebuilt and thrives today. Other owners of the building were the proprietors of a pub restauarant dubbed appropriately "The Station"; this has since disappeared and, at the time of writing, the premises are up for sale-something the current political climate would seem to favour. *W.A.Brown*

Broadbottom (for Mottram and Charlesworth), July 1971: Viewed from the footbridge (bridge 49), this was the original station building sited on the Up side of the line. A splendid three-storey structure in the Italianate style, the building looks as if it could be equally at home in the foothills of the Alps! Aside from the intrusion of the catenary and alterations to the fine-looking chimneys, little has changed on this side of the line in the intervening years since the pre-1923 picture was taken. Later rebuilding would see an outer wall added under the platform canopy. Were the rather glum-looking passengers waiting for their EMU in need, perhaps, of one of the "wonderful summer weekends in London" portrayed on the platform advertisement board? In 1963 a second class return from here to Manchester Piccadilly (or Central) cost just 2/11d. For those wishing to venture to Oxford Road a further 2d. was charged! *W.A.Brown*

Mottram and Broadbottom, n.d: The title "Great Central Railway" on the platform hoardings marks this out as a true pre-Group view. There is much to delight the station enthusiast here-what wonderful prospects for a model! Aside from the splendid Italianate building with those wonderful chimneys, the delicate lattice footbridge and accompanying single-arch overbridge (bridge 48 carrying Moss Lane over the GCR main line), are delights in themselves. The platform shelter on the Down (left-hand side of the line) was replaced by the present wooden building by the LNER in 1931. What a shame we cannot see a Great Central Atlantic storming under the road bridge; still, we can content ourselves with the sight of the superb MS&L-style gas lamps with their most ornate and unique bulb-shaped base, fluted column and fine top. Whatever happened to style? *Collection of Brian Hilton*

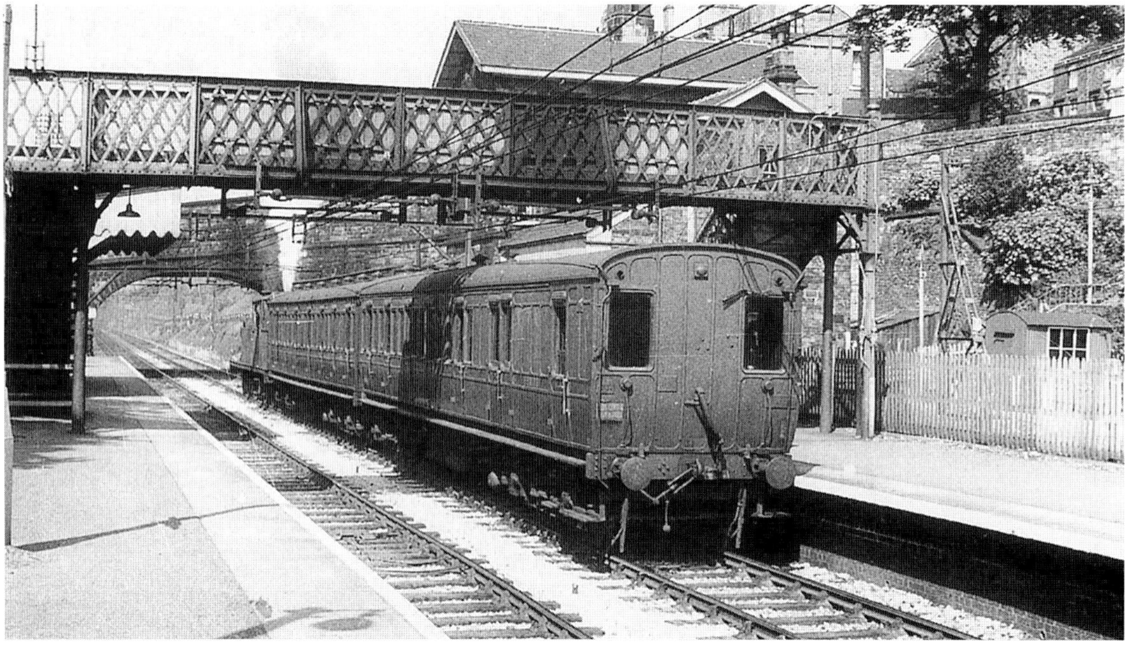

Broadbottom (for Mottram and Charlesworth), June 5th.1954: History is made at Broadbottom with the sight of this Manchester London Road to Glossop push-pull train, hauled (or rather, pushed) by C13 No.**67421**. Today, Saturday, sees the last day of steam on the Glossop and Hadfield services. Come next week and the 1500v Dc EMU sets will transform the local passenger workings-a transformation indeed from such antediluvian scenes such as this. *D.Chatfield*

Leaving Broadbottom station the gradient of the Woodhead line steepens from 1-in-462 to 1-in-122. Past milepost 10 and the land appears to suddenly fall away revealing a great chasm in the earth. This is the void formed by the River Etherow meandering here some 120 feet below rail level. Before closure beyond Hadfield this sudden vista would have acted as an hors d'oeuvre for the scenic pleasures yet to come as the wild Pennine scenery began to unfold before the traveller's eyes.

Mottram viaduct was constructed initially in 1842 and was opened for traffic with due ceremony on Christmas Eve the same year. Referred to in earlier literature as "Etherow Viaduct" the structure, like its neighbour spanning Dinting Vale, was built out of timber. Joseph Locke, the Engineer-in-Chief of the SA&M, is credited with the design of the three-arch viaduct, though Alfred Jee prepared the drawings. No less than 186,00 cu.ft. of stone, quarried locally at neighbouring Tintwistle. 41,00 cu.ft.of timber were absorbed in the building of the arches. But, as at Dinting, the timber spans did not last long and reconstruction was required in 1860. This time wrought iron box outer girders were used. Further strengthening took place in 1894 when two steel fish bellied inner girders were added. The most noticeable alteration in modern times took place in 1918-20 when three brick piers were added to divide the spans. This work cost a total of £16,266 and was carried out by John Moffat & Co. of Manchester. Interestingly, a scheme had been hatched around that time to quadruple the line by building another viaduct, carrying the Fast lines, alongside the earlier one. A total span of 422'-6" is recorded in the official bridge register.

Mottram Viaduct, November 23rd.1955: A lot of water has passed under this particular bridge in the interim; to say nothing of many, many trains over it. An official photograph, this view shows clearly the alterations carried out just after the First World War when the three brick strengthening piers were inserted. Electrification has now arrived on the scene too and the bridge was altered yet again in 1939 when the cross girders were renewed. It isn't just locomotives that require replacement! Aperiod touch is provided by the sight of the RAC-sponsored road sign in the bottom left-hand corner informing drivers that they are entering the village of Broadbottom. *British Railways*

Mottram Viaduct, 19th.Century: The second viaduct which was constructed in 1860. Originally, three arched timber spans filled the spaces where the wrought iron box girders can be seen. The two visible piers would have been part of Locke's original structure dating from 1842. *Collection of R.P.Hepner*

Mottram Yard, 1935: A view showing the king points and control tower from which they and the further points leading to the sorting sidings beyond were operated. The buildings beyond the control tower comprised various yard offices. *British Railways*

MOTTRAM AND DINTING MARSHALLING YARD, L.N.E.R.

(Reproduced from The Railway Gazette-October 18th.1935)

The former Great Central main line between Penistone and Manchester forms the sole means of access over L.N.E.R. metals to the important manufacturing centres in Lancashire and Cheshire and to the districts served by the Cheshire Lines, the Wigan and St.Helens branches, and the Chester, Wrexham and Birkenhead lines. There is a very heavy volume of goods and mineral traffic over this main line from places east of Woodhead to places west of Godley, Guide Bridge and Manchester. This traffic is either transferred to the Cheshire Lines at Godley, or passes through Guide Bridge, whence booked services of trains are run to the points of exchange with the Western, Midland and Central sections of the L.M.S.R. as well as to the Cheshire Lines and beyond via Fallowfield.

The existing sidings at Guide Bridge are quite unsuitable for sorting and marshalling the large number of wagons which pass through them, and the accommodation is inadequate. The layout of the yard is such that a considerable amount of transfer is entailed between two groups of sidings which involves the crossing of the main lines. In order that the traffic be dealt with more expeditiously and economically, it became essential that there should be provided, at a point as near as possible to Guide Bridge, a new marshalling yard, into which trains conveying down traffic could be run clear of the main lines and re-formed into through trains for particular destinations.

Topographical Engineering Difficulties

As this main line passes through the very rugged country of the Pennine Range, involving many sharp curves and severe gradients, it was exceedingly difficult to find a suitable location for a marshalling yard. A site between Dinting and Mottram, about 11 miles from Manchester, and within easy distance of Godley and Guide Bridge, was finally selected as being the most practical from an engineering point of view. The scheme involved a diversion of the main line for a length of about three-quarters of a mile, and the acquisition of a large area of land, and Parliamentary powers for these were obtained in 1930: the work is now virtually completed.

The Yards Described

The new marshalling yard is situated on the down side of the main line, and covers a distance of 1 mile 26 ch. The inlet to the yard is from the down main line at the Dinting end, where there are eight reception sidings, each holding a train of 80 wagons. These sidings are on a falling gradient of 1 in 85 towards the sorting sidings, as will be seen from the plan and gradient profile reproduced, and they are also illustrated. The sorting layout consists of two groups of 10 sidings, each holding 65 wagons and is also illustrated: the sorting of traffic for various destinations is effected by gravity. The points leading into the various roads are electrically controlled and are operated by pneumatic power. The sorting sidings are grouped together at the Mottram end into a common departure road leading to the main line. An avoiding line for engines from the reception roads to the main line, and lying between the sorting sidings and the main line is provided. Two sidings, each to hold 30 wagons, are available for crippled wagons, together with sidings for brake vans and a short siding for cattle traffic, two cattle pens being provided.

Offices for the yard master and accommodation for the shunting staff are provided near the entrance to the sorting sidings and are also illustrated. Provision has also been made for a possible future widening of the main line.

Engineering Works Involved

Although the site selected was the best that could be found, it involved a considerable amount of heavy excavation work. The diversion of the existing main line is mostly on embankment which has a maximum height of 90 ft. the construction of this embankment proved very difficult owing (a) to the unstable nature of the material excavated from the cuttings, which was tipped to form the embankment, and (b) to the fact that the foundation was largely on silt, overlying rock at a depth of approximately

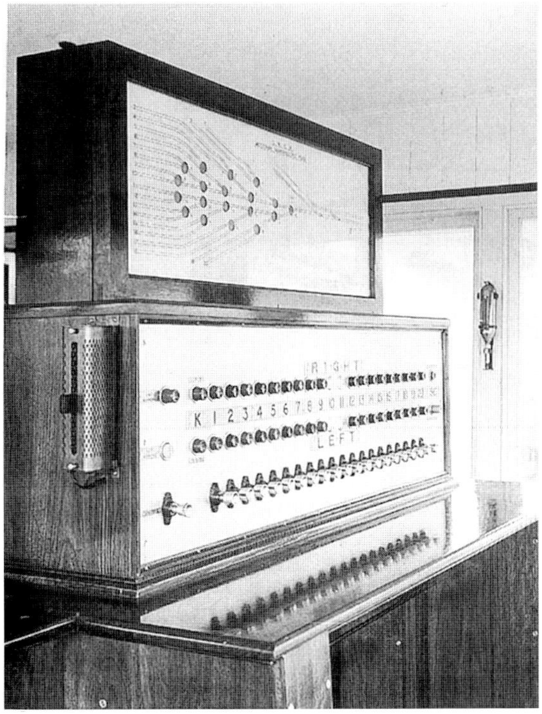

Mottram Yard, June 23rd.1957: The yard in modern times with electric traction reigning supreme. The view looks east to Dinting from the Glossop Road overbridge. Below are the Reception Sidings, entrance to which was controlled by Mottram Yard No.2 signalbox sited round the curve. Passing along the Up main line is a 10-coach express with the now usual EM1 or EM2 locomotive at its head. Through a vista of overhead line supports the yard looks busy; open wagons, some wooden-bodied, abound-with containers loaded onto on flat wagons well to the fore.
D.Chatfield

40 ft., which silt constantly subsided and tended to move forward under the superimposed weight. During the construction it was found necessary to drive a length of sheet piling down to the rock, across the lowest part of the valley, in order to stop the movement, and to construct, behind the piling, a heavy concrete retaining wall, actually 20 ft.thick, to retain the toe of the embankment. The upper 20 ft. of the embankment was formed with ashes to minimise the additional load on the foundation. An old culvert passing under the original bank carrying the railway, which had been badly affected by an old slip, had to be reconstructed for the greater part of its length and also extended, before the new embankment was tipped.

The maximum depth of the cutting is 80 ft., the angle of slope being 2½ horiozontal to 1 vertical owing to the nature of the strata. Altogether approximately 1,250,000 cu. yd. of material were excavated of which 329,000 cu. yd. were used in forming the embankment, with an addition of 85,000 cu. yd. of ashes. The remainder was tipped to spoil alongside the new yard.

An important main road, known as Glossop Road*, is carried over the railway by means of a viaduct which had to be extended: its centre opening is a steel girder span, while the six side spans are arches. This viaduct crosses the railway at a point midway between the reception and sorting sidings at a height of 55 ft. above rail level, and the views reproduced of these two groups of sidings are from it, one from each side. Originally a stone-faced viaduct of five spans, it was reconstructed and widened to provide a roadway 40 ft. between parapets. Two of the five arches at the southern end of the old structure were removed and a steel span substituted; beyond it three additional brick arched spans being added as may be seen in the illustration. The main opening through which the sidings pass is 80 ft. 4 in. between piers and the length of the viaduct was increased from 230 to 380 ft.

At the Mottram end of the yard a road, known as Botany Lane, passes under the railway to a calico printing mill. A new bridge of 20 ft. span with steel superstructure and brick abutments was constructed to carry the diverted main line, the original bridge, a brick arch of the same span, being extended for a distance of 36 ft. in order to carry the departure sidings from the new yard.

When the yard is in full operation, betwen 40 and 50 engines will take water during a day. Unfortunately, there was not a sufficient supply of water available in the district to meet the new demand, so water had to be obtained from a well which has been sunk to a depth of 300 ft. The bore has a diameter of 15 in. and water is pumped from it into a storage tank of 50,000 gallons capacity.

Method of Operation

The operation of the yard is on the gravity principle. Trains arriving from the east enter the reception sidings and from them they are sectionalised into twenty sorting sidings for their various destinations in the Manchester district. The reception sidings are on a falling gradient of 1 in 85 from east to west. At the western end of these sidings is a short length of single track lying on a gradient of 1 in 30, falling. This gives a wagon, or a group of wagons, running down it the necessary acceleration to carry it (or them) into the required sorting siding. The sorting sidings themselves lie on a falling gradient, 1 in 75, to commence with, flattening out to 1 in 200 at the lower or western end, so that the speed of the wagons may be reduced gradually as they travel through the siding and come to rest before fouling the adjoining sidings at the outgoing end.

Telephonic Communications to Direct Control Operator

An operator in the control tower, illustrated, near the eastern entrance to the sorting sidings operates electric pushes working the points for directing each wagon, or group of wagons, into the particular sorting sidings allocated to its destination. He will be informed by the shunter through loud-speaking telephone-operated from four transmitters at the top of the 1 in 30 gradient, as the wagon or wagons are uncoupled-the destination siding thereof. When a train in the reception sidings is ready for re-marshalling, the train is allowed to move forward slowly by gravity, a shunter stationed at the top of the incline uncoupling each wagon, or group of wagons, as they pass, and telephoning their siding destination as previously explained. Experiments are also being made with a double-sided indicator to display visually the siding destination of the wagons and so confirm to the ground staff the destinations of the various weagons telephoned to the control tower, the indications being set up automatically when the pushes operating the respective points are depressed.

Points Control

In the control tower is a control panel consisting of a row of push buttons and an illuminated diagram to indicate the movement of each wagon, or group of wagons, generally known to the operators as a cut. Each push button, when operated, sets up a complete route to one of the sidings in the sorting yard from the reception sidings, and the operator, knowing the destination of each cut, is able to operate the push buttons in the proper sequence so as to direct each cut to the correct sidings. As each cut passes over the king points near the control tower, the route button for the following cut is pressed and the route for that cut in turn is stored up in the mechanism and eventually set automatically by the passing of the previous cut.

Compressed Air System

The points are operated by compressed air, which is controlled from the tower by means of electrically-operated valves, and each pair of points is held during the passing of the cuts by means of an electric track circuit, which also operates the apparatus for automatic point operation referred to above. The air supply is obtained from a compressor plant at Dog Lane power station and is conveyed by a pipe line to two reserve tanks outside the Mottram control tower. The pressure is there reduced from 35 lb. to 20 lb. per sq. in. for point operation. A small electrically driven standby compressor is provided under the control tower, which can be started up in the event of a failure of the main air pipe line. The supply to the yard is taken over a ring air main provided with isolating valves so that any pipe defect can be handled with a minimum interference with the point operations and delay to traffic.

**Glossop Road is referred to an older maps as "Gamesley Road."*

Mottram Yard, June 24th.1935: A panoramic view of the sorting sidings looking westwards from the Glossop Road overbridge. The main line is at a higher level and can be seen on the extreme right. The two siding grids, each of 10 roads, can be identified splitting from the king points in the foreground. Truly a massive project and one that could only have been undertaken when the railways were still the nation's major freight haulers. *British Railways*

Mottram Yard, 1935: The reception sidings, with the main line to the left, viewed from the Glossop Road overbridge and looking east towards Dinting. The copious earthworks required and the extent of the yard can be clearly seen. When the yard was being built, the GCR main line was re-aligned and straightened out. The new alignment took a path some sixty yards north of its previous position. Visible in the background on the left is the goods yard at Old Dinting-the original Dinting station site-and beyond this the entry to the Waterside Mill branch. *British Railways*

Mottram Yard, 1935: The Glossop Road overbridge, known locally as "Gamesley Bridge", seen as extended to span the main line-set off at a higher level on the left-and the the two roads connecting the reception and sorting sidings, at a lower level, on the right. The central girder span accommodates the connecting roads. As stated construction of the yard caused the alignment of the main line to be altered; a reverse curve was removed and the line straightened to make way for the new construction.

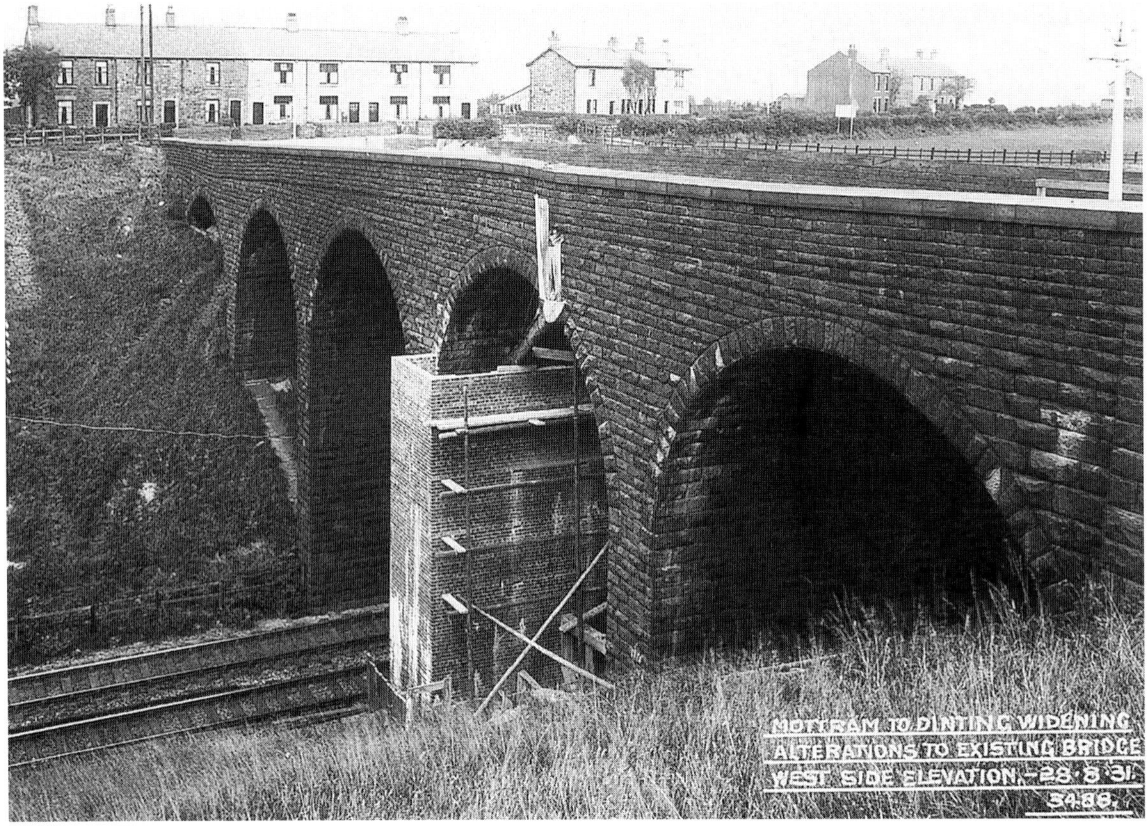

Mottram Yard, Glossop Road bridge-August 28th.1931: Preliminary work on bridge No.53 is well advanced. Engineers have cased in the stone pier on the south side of the main line which can be seen passing beneath the third arch. Following on this the massive excavation exercise will proceed and huge steel girders will be lowered into place to form a 79 ft. 6 in. span between the piers spanning the siding roads. Notice the chute in place from road level to deliver materials into the void between the brickwork and the stone facing of the old viaduct.

British Railways

Mottram Yard, 1935: The bridge is complete-a fascinating contrast with the previous picture and a superb example of the civil engineer's expertise. Looking at the perfect alignment of the hundreds of thousands of bricks forming the new structure it is easy to empathise with the bricklayer who, reputedly, stated that.."plumbing, joinery and plastering were mere trades; but bricklaying was an art!"

British Railways

Mottram Yard, June 12th.1954: The last weekend of steam on the Woodhead line, at least west of Penistone, sees 3F 0-6-0 No.43793 engaged in shunting work at the east end of the yard. The platforms on the main line in the background served as a trainmen's halt for staff deployed in the yard complex. Despite closure beginning in 1967 the modern day working timetable has continued to show a service to this halt from Manchester Piccadilly! *Tom Lewis*

Mottram Yard, April 21st.1951: Austerity 2-8-0 No.90435 of Hull Dairycoates looks thoroughly unloved and unkempt as it slogs eastwards towards Dinting with an Up freight. Down below, the sprawl of Mottram Yard serves to underline the point that this railway, more than anything else, was about the movement of freight. Notice on the lineside that supporting posts and brackets are in place ready for the high voltage feeder cables for the electrification programme. Much remains to be done overhead, though a forest of steel supports heralds the day, still over three years off, when scenes like this will be but a memory. *B.K.B.Green*

Mottram Yard, August 1967: Upset at Mottram. The signalman at Mottram No.1 certainly had problems when Bo-Bo No.**26053** *Perseus* left the rails and keeled over causing its train of loaded coal wagons to pile up behind. Blocked completely are the two roads in and out of the yard and the shunting neck behind, though with a crowd of some 15 railwaymen on hand the breakdown crew would not have been short of advice. The presence of so much "overhead" in situations like this tended to cause problems for manouvering of the crane's jib. *Reporter Group of Newspapers*

Mottram Yard, June 12th.1954: Last day of steam on the Woodhead line. The district of Gamesley is glimpsed as Gorton-based K3 No.61910 passes the eastern extremity of the yard with a Doncaster to Manchester train. Off to the right can be seen part of the reception sidings; the photographer stands at the end of a ¼ mile long shunting neck that paralleled the Down main line. Mottram No.2 signalbox which controlled operations to and from this end of the yard is visible in the background. This box, and neighbouring Mottram No.1 dated from the opening of the yard; they replaced two previous boxes: Old Dinting and Mottram Station.
Tom Lewis

The Derbyshire town of Glossop developed around the traditional northern industries of weaving and textile production-cotton and its associated cloth, calico. To serve the complex of mills at Waterside-near to the River Etherow and sited between Hadfield and Tintwistle, north-west of Glossop-the MS&L opened a 2 mile, 16 chains branch from the old Dinting station. The line was built under powers obtained via an Act of 1874 and opened for traffic in 1879.

From Old Dinting goods yard the steeply graded (much at 1-in-40) Waterside line crossed the Glossop to Marple road (A626) via a level crossing (the gates of which still survive today). The line then crossed the valley near to the Roman Fort of Melandra Castle before bridging the A57 Manchester to Sheffield road at Brookfield, near to Woolley Bridge.

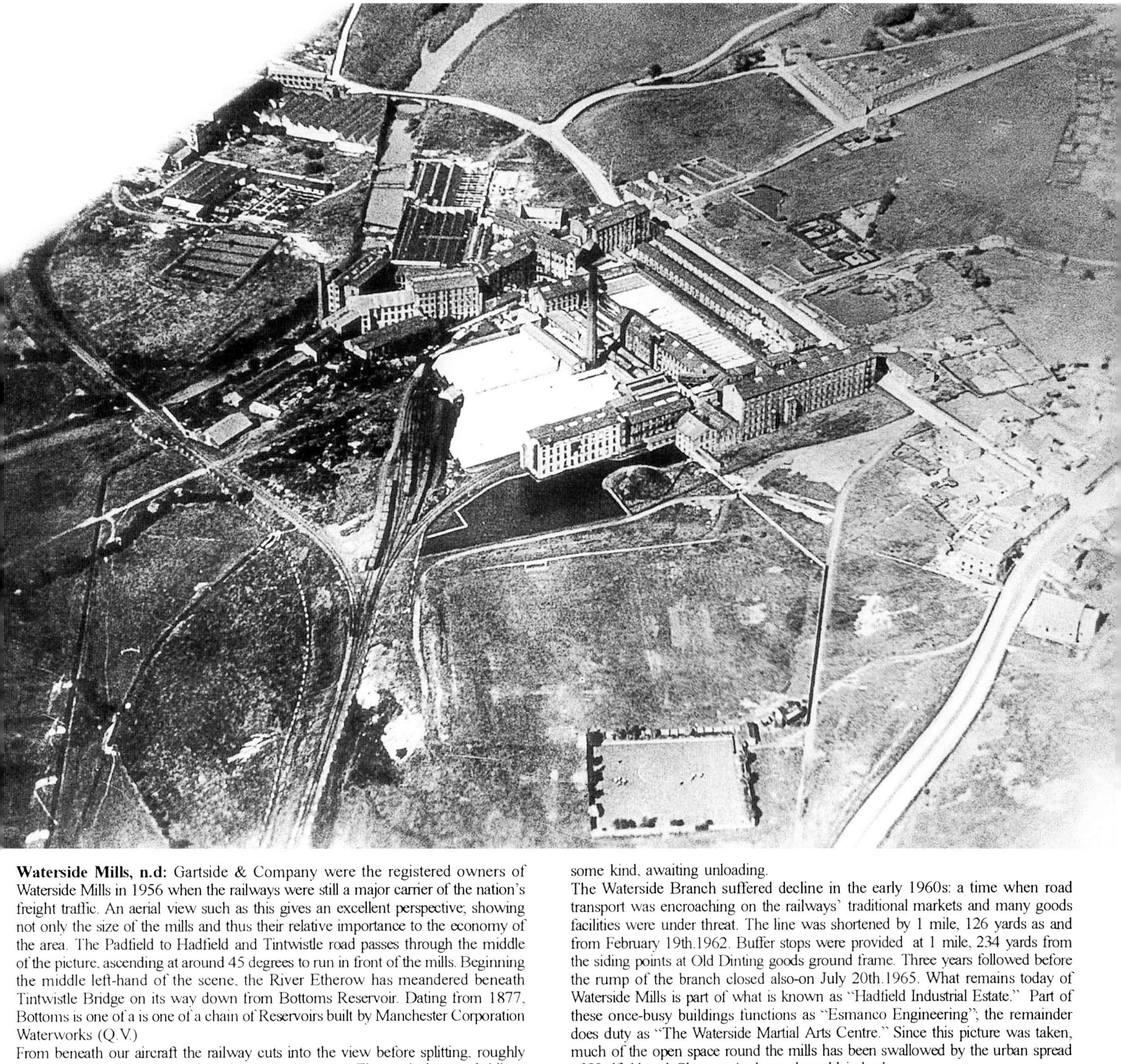

Waterside Mills, n.d: Gartside & Company were the registered owners of Waterside Mills in 1956 when the railways were still a major carrier of the nation's freight traffic. An aerial view such as this gives an excellent perspective; showing not only the size of the mills and thus their relative importance to the economy of the area. The Padfield to Hadfield and Tintwistle road passes through the middle of the picture, ascending at around 45 degrees to run in front of the mills. Beginning the middle left-hand of the scene, the River Etherow has meandered beneath Tintwistle Bridge on its way down from Bottoms Reservoir. Dating from 1877, Bottoms is one of a is one of a chain of Reservoirs built by Manchester Corporation Waterworks (Q.V.)
From beneath our aircraft the railway cuts into the view before splitting, roughly in the middle of the picture, into three separate arms. The vertical row of sidings appears to be the busiest with some 24 open wagons, possibly coal or minerals of some kind, awaiting unloading.
The Waterside Branch suffered decline in the early 1960s: a time when road transport was encroaching on the railways' traditional markets and many goods facilities were under threat. The line was shortened by 1 mile, 126 yards as and from February 19th.1962. Buffer stops were provided at 1 mile, 234 yards from the siding points at Old Dinting goods ground frame. Three years followed before the rump of the branch closed also-on July 20th.1965. What remains today of Waterside Mills is part of what is known as "Hadfield Industrial Estate." Part of these once-busy buildings functions as "Esmanco Engineering"; the remainder does duty as "The Waterside Martial Arts Centre." Since this picture was taken, much of the open space round the mills has been swallowed by the urban spread of Hadfield and Glossop. A changed world indeed.

Glossop Heritage Centre collection

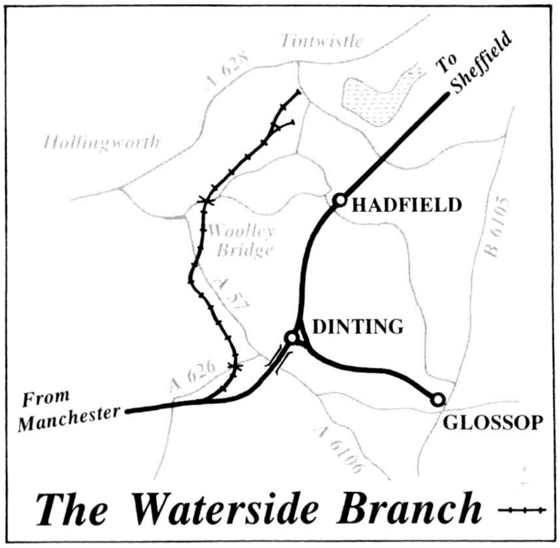

Waterside Mill Branch, May 5th.1959: On this day a trip was made down the branch by a party from the Railway Enthusiasts' Club. This view of the bridge near to Melandra Castle was taken as the 3-coach special, hauled by Standard 2-6-4 Tank No.**80044**, headed back towards Old Dinting.
Brian Hilton

Waterside Mill Branch, n.d: This was the view at Brookfield showing the bridge carrying the branch over the A57-Manchester to Sheffield-road. The photographer is looking towards Glossop, Woolley Bridge is behind. With the bridge dropped in recent years, the scene here has changed out of all recognition. The embankments have been removed and, just to the left, newly-created Tavern Road, with its pretty little new houses, now stands.
Glossop Heritage Centre collection

Dinting station, August 6th 1951. B1 No **61145** comes off the viaduct and enters Dinting Station with a nine-coach Up special working, reporting number 334. Electrification is still some way off although catenary support gantries are in place. A lineside group pauses from its task to watch the express roar past on its journey east, such is the powerful fascination of moving trains. In the foreground, the well worn timbers of another railway tradition, the barrow crossing, reminds us of the numerous facilities that one took for granted on a railway station. The modern railway of the 1990s has rendered these crossings almost obsolete, but the ease of access to stations and their services must surely be of some importance to any would be commercial undertaking, safety permitting.
Gordan Coltas

Dintings Viaduct on the G.C R Main Line between Manchester and Sheffield. Length, 1,200 feet; height, 130 feet.

Dinting Viaduct: Reproduced from a nineteenth century publication, this is a view from the station side looking towards Mottram and Broadbottom. The viaduct is seen in its second phase: minus the original timber central section but without the later brick strengthening piers. Notice the exposed nature of the arches on the Mottram side. *Author's collection*

DINTING VIADUCT

Almost immediately after passing Mottram Yard No.2 signalbox the main line crossed Dinting Vale by means of a lengthy viaduct; arguably the most impressive bridge, though not necessarily structure, on the whole Woodhead route. As at nearby Mottram, construction of the viaduct dated from the line's early days and, in like manner, replacement of timber by more durable materials took place within two decades of the line's opening (1860).

Dinting Vale viaduct comprises three sections: running in an easterly direction from Mottram is a series of seven stone arches each 50 ft. wide and 22 ft.10 in. between the parapets. The central section consists of five openings (later divided by strengthening piers). A further four stone arches, each, again, 50 ft.wide takes the railway to the westerly junction with the Glossop branch and into Dinting station.

The replacement, in 1860, of the original timber central structure was undertaken using wrought iron box girders and fish-bellied inner girders. Strengthening took place initially in 1894 when steel was used in the shape of two steel inner girders.

In like fashion to Mottram viaduct, the most noticeable changes to the structure occurred between 1918-1920 when seven brick strengthening piers were added. Though an obvious necessity, the aesthetic appearance of the earlier rebuilding was somewhat spoilt. Bricking-up of many of the stone arches has, in like manner, taken away the early architectural beauty.

Dinting Vale viaduct is a total of just 1200 feet wide. Of this, the central section (openings nos.8-12) takes up a combined width of just over half the total-at 650 ft. 6 in. Maximum headway is recorded officially as 119 feet, though early literature gives this as 130 feet. Major repairs were carried out in 1939 when the cross girders were renewed. Even in 1996, when travel has broadened many minds and opened up vistas and horizons undreamed of in the 1840s, the view from the viaduct on a clear day is still a breathtaking one. Passing along the A57 Sheffield road beneath the myriad of brick, stone and steel this splendid piece of Victorian civil engineering is yet a thing to wonder at. Long may we be able to do so.

Dinting Viaduct, 1954: Taken in immediate pre-electrification days this panorama looks west from a similar vantage point to the early view. Notice how the brick piers crowd the space between the original stone ones and see how the ground has been raised around the seven stone arches-all of which are now filled in. The trains seem diminutive-almost appearing like models and completely out of proportion to their means of support. On the Up line an unidentified B1 hauls a clean-looking train of carmine and cream-liveried coaches in the direction of Dinting station. Just clearing the viaduct on the opposite track yet another loose-coupled freight ambles along towards Mottram Yard. In the second of the original openings from the left the A57 Sheffield road runs in the direction of Glossop. The footbridge in the near foreground was given over to Glossop Corporation in 1965. *B.K.B.Green*

Dinting Viaduct, July 15th.1972: Raymond Keeley's close-up study of the viaduct reveals interesting details not apparent in our longer views: clearly visible are the cast iron shoes that held the original timber arches on the massive bedstones (or imposts) seen below the box girders. Doubtless Raymond's two sons, Michael and Patrick, had to be distracted from the passing EM1 (then Class 76) Bo-Bo heading for Mottram Yard to enable him to incorporate them in his picture! *Raymond Keeley*

Dinting Viaduct, 1957: This was the view as seen only by the Motorman and his assistant as their trains passed high over Dinting Vale-a breathtaking maximum of 119 feet above the ground. Small wonder that staff had to be forbidden to use the viaduct as a shortcut to reach Mottram Yard! A train of vans rushes towards us, but before we leave the viaduct several features can be discerned: for a start, the permanent way is laid in a totally different fashion to that on solid ground. Notice the chairs supporting the bullhead rails are fixed to longitudinal timbers; a continuous check rail, fixed 1¾" inside of the running rail is provided throughout the length of the viaduct. Spacing the timbers apart are bolted transoms acting as anchors to maintain the gauge. Such features are reminiscent of Brunel's "baulk road" laid to 7'-0¼" gauge for the original Great Western line. The pillasters with their ornamental capstones correspond to the original stone piers and provide a key to the location: here we are approaching the west side of the viaduct and are within sight of Mottram Yard-the No.2 box is just visible on the horizon. *B.K.B.Green*

Dinting Station, July 17th.1971: A splendid view of the Down main line platform buildings and adjacent signalbox-a picture taken when lighting conditions were well nigh perfect and able to highlight the architectural splendour of the Victorian buildings. This magnificent structure, with its fretted bargeboards and fine stone lintels dated from 1884 when a package of measures-including enlargement of the station and associated facilities, the triangular junction with the Glossop line and provision of double track along the 1 mile branch-were put into place. The ample accommodation on offer here has provided a home for the Permanent Way Inspector, the Station Master and the usual range of first and second class waiting rooms. Truly, the Victorians did nothing by halves. Notice how the overhead line mast has been skilfully incorporated into the slated platform canopy. *W.A.Brown*

Dinting Station, May 9th.1953: Viewed from the station footbridge B1 No.61190 passes cautiously through Dinting's main line platforms with the 9.43 a.m. Cleethorpes to Manchester express. This service, conveying a Buffet Car, made three stops after leaving Sheffield Victoria-at Penistone, Dunford Bridge and Guide Bridge. Arrival in Manchester (London Road) was at 1.25. The station approach road on the far left-hand side extends from Dinting Road and its companion piece, the fine stone overbridge (No.56), dates from 1884. Some splendid examples of "railwayana"-MS&L period lamps and cast iron signs help to give this view a vintage flavour. Dinting station signalbox still carries its LNER nameboard. *B.K.B.Green*

Dinting, c.1953: A J11 0-6-0 runs tender-first into Dinting with an Up stopping train bound for Hadfield. Though of endless fascination to the enthusiast, the demise of steam-hauled local workings,coupled with the arrival of the new EMUs brought a big upsurge in suburban travel over the Manchester-Glossop-Hadfield route. In the first few months of suburban electrification passenger receipts were reported as being up by 125%. The siding on the left ran round from the alongside the engine shed and lay adjacent to a coal stacking ground for local merchants. Ahead is Dinting Viaduct and beyond was Mottram Yard. The sign on the left warns that:"Staff proceeding for duty at Mottram Yard must not use the viaduct but must proceed by the roadway." Hardly surprising considering the exposed nature of the location, to say nothing of the long drop! The Glossop branch cuts in at the bottom left-hand corner of the picture; notice the single catch tongue ("catch point") where the Up Branch leaves the main line. This was designed to deflect errant vehicles away from danger; the last $^{1}/_{8}$ mile or so of the branch fell at 1-in-187 to 1-in-100 towards this point. *H.Townley*

A station had existed at Dinting from the earliest days of the SAuL&M. Trains first reached this place on December 24th.1842; in those early days the station was named "Glossop" and was the terminus of the embryo line. From here a coach and horses took the traveller on to Sheffield, bringing the journey time between the two cities to just five hours.

On June 9th.1845 the one mile branch to Glossop, a single line, opened for goods traffic. The branch had been built as a private line for the Duke of Norfolk and thus had required no Act of Parliament. Despite this, the railway was worked by the SAuL&M from the beginning- although Parliamentary powers had to be obtained in the 1846 session to enable the company to take it over from the Duke. Passenger traffic to Glossop began on June 30th.1845 whereupon the erstwhile "Glossop" station became known as "Dinting." Glossop Station was re-named "Glossop Central" on July 10th.1922. The original connection from the Glossop branch to the main line was by means of a facing connection from the Sheffield end of the line. A temporary wooden structure with a covered platform existed here from October 1845 at what was termed "Glossop Junction". A more permanent structure was built by Messrs.Chadwick and France for the sum of £496.15/- and was opened on February 1st.1847. The name "Dinting" seems to have been used from early days, although an (undated) MS&L official plan refers to the station as "Dinting Junction Station." Plain "Dinting" appears to have been dropped by 1922 in favour of "Glossop and Dinting" before reverting to "Dinting" in modern times.

The original Dinting station had been sited ¾ mile nearer to Manchester on the west side of Dinting Viaduct. Upon the opening of the permanent station at the junction with the Glossop Branch this early station was renamed "Old Dinting" and was used for goods traffic only. From this point the branch to Waterside Mill serving local industries began - opening in 1879.

Under the MS&L Railway (additional powers) Act of 1883 the branch to Glossop was doubled and an east to south curve was laid at Dinting from the Glossop Branch to the main line just east of the viaduct. A single-road engine shed and coaling stage was provided at Dinting; this nestled on the south side of the east to south curve and was accessed from the Glossop branch at a point just by Dinting Lane level crossing. It was this engine shed and adjacent site that was for many years the home of the Bahamas Locomotive Society and made the name of "Dinting" synonymous with modern-day preservation. Sadly, the site of the Dinting Railway Centre, as it was known, has long been cleared and the preservationists are no more. The shed still exists intact, a sole reminder of locomotive activity here.

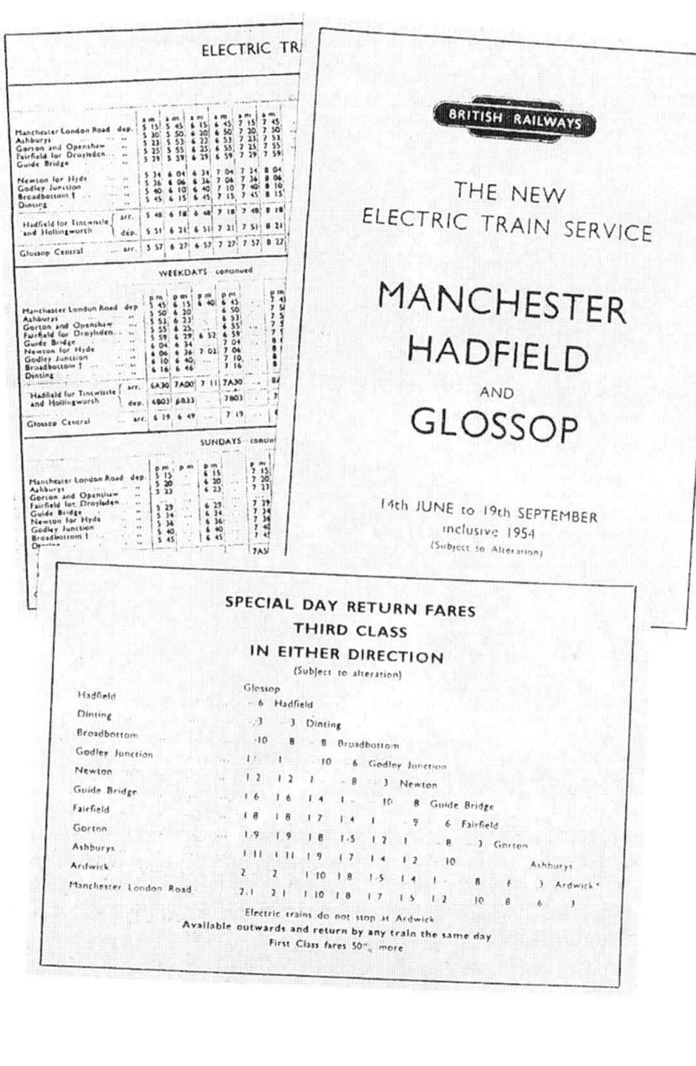

Dinting Station, 1954: C13 No.**67417** pauses in the Glossop Branch platform with a push-pull working to Manchester London Road. The train is on the curve installed in 1884 (under the 1883 Additional Powers Act) enabling direct connection with Glossop from the Manchester direction and making a triangular junction at Dinting. Notice the very sharp curve complete with continuous check rail. The platform faces have been rebuilt to provide clearance for the forthcoming EMUs; notice also the centre section of the footbridge has been boarded in to prevent stray contact with the overhead electric line. Before we leave Dinting it is timely to reflect on the contrast between steam and electric working as they affected local services here. The 1938 timetable shows a regular weekday service of 21 stopping trains between Manchester London Road and Glossop. A journey immediately pre-War took 38-45 minutes and a service of 21 regular weekday trains was provided. Electrification in 1954 offered a regular interval service-at 2 minutes and 32 minutes past the hour from Glossop respectively taking 32 minutes for the journey into Manchester.
Harry Townley/J.M.Bentley collection

Approaching Dinting Station, May 8th.1954: The name "Dinting" will long be associated with the Bahamas Locomotive Society who made their home here on the site of the former engine shed in the 1970s. Approaching Dinting Station and passing the entry to the engine shed is motor-fitted C13 No.**67421** with a Glossop to Manchester London Road push-pull train. This would be the last year of such antiquarian workings and, though, regretted by the enthusiast, such scenes would soon be a thing of the past. Push-pull working of the Manchester to Glossop and Hadfield local services had begun in the early 1930s with F1 2-4-2 Tank engines of 1890s vintage. The footbridge in the background was adjacent to a level crossing once under the control of a signalbox known as "Dinting South." An LNER (Southern Area) map dated January 1st.1931 shows this signalbox "dispensed with" and the associated gate locks, points to the loco yard, headshunt and adjacent crossover as being worked electrically from the signalbox at Dinting Station ("Glossop & Dinting Signal Box"). 67421 has just crossed the pointwork of the entrance to the loco shed; access to this was from the Up line (i.e.Glossop direction) only. *B.K.B.Green*

Between Hadfield and Glossop May 8th.1954: O4/7 No.**63708** pauses on the curve round from the north-east of Dinting Station to Glossop. The driver finds time to roll a cigarette while a plume of steam lifts from the safety valves; this was still very much the day and age of the loose-coupled freight train-coal and empties bound for the yard at Glossop, just along the branch. Notice the splitting Home signals in the background with the 10 m.p.h.speed restriction governing both directions of working: left round to Dinting Station in the direction of Manchester and right towards Hadfield and Sheffield. *B.K.B.Green*

Dinting Station, looking north-west, September 16th.1956: A view taken from the top of the cutting above the Glossop Branch-seen in the bottom left-hand corner. Here we are standing just above where the 04 and its goods train were waiting-seen in a previous photograph. The line ahead continues to Hadfield avoiding Dinting Station; whilst to the left is the 1884 curve which joins the main line where the J11 was seen with the local train. In the top background can be seen the main line to Hadfield, the station buildings at Dinting and the signalbox.
J.W.F.Scrimgeour/courtesy Signalling Record Society

Dinting Station Signalbox, interior, September 16th.1956: A good view of a GCR "Jug Handle" lever frame-a distinctive pattern manufactured for the company by a variety of contractors including the Railway Signal Co., Mc.Kenzie & Holland, Saxby & Farmer and Westinghouse. The illuminated diagram over the frame shows the layout at Dinting: notice the loop on the Up line in the Hadfield direction and the two gradient diagrams: rising to Hadfield and generally falling towards Glossop. On the block shelf can be seen LNER standard block instruments, that on the left controls the section from Mottram No.2, those on the right are for the sections to Glossop and Hadfield. Below the diagram are the repeaters for the various signals-a mixture of colour lights and semaphores in those days. On the levers themselves engraved plastic plates (black on white) show the lever descriptions and the numbers of corresponding levers that must be pulled first to release the locking. Two examples are worth a glance: No.11-"Down Main/Down Branch" and No.18 "Down Branch to Manchester Starting 33 11 Line Clear"-in simple terms meaning a Starting signal for the Manchester direction requiring levers Nos.33 and 11 to be pulled first and a "line clear" showing on the offering block instrument to Mottram No.2 before the signal could be released. *J.W.F.Scrimgeour courtesy Signalling Record Society*

Dinting Engine Shed, n.d: This is the part of Dinting that will be most familiar to modern-day enthusiasts: the engine shed and adjacent yard that were once the home of the Bahamas Locomotive Society. Confusion seems to surround the origin and existence of this one-time locomotive depot. An LNER map of uncertain date shows the shed and surrounding area and is marked:"proposed re-opening of Dinting Loco.Shed." One source reports that the shed had closed in 1938; whether closure had occurred at an earlier stage in the shed's history is not known. As a sub-shed of Gorton, Dinting had no fixed allocation of engines of its own. Though comprising the usual basic facilities of coaling and watering, Dinting had no boiler wash-out facilities and these ablutions had to be undertaken at the parent shed. Whatever closure may have occurred in previous years,in this scene electric and steam locos seem alive and well and co-existing at Dinting; A Bo-Bo has dutifully stopped in front of the sign reading:"ELEC.LOCOS STOP HERE." J11/3 No.**64332** is making an exit from the single road shed alongside the coaling stage. To the side of the tender a young man, possibly the fireman, can be seen-a shovel appears on the J11's tender. Round the corner, an O4 2-8-0 awaits its next turn of duty. *H.Townley*

Between Dinting and Glossop, May 8th.1954: For many enthusiasts the C13 4-4-2 tank engines were amongst the last of the former Great Central engines that they were familiar with. In the final full month of steam working on the London Road to Glossop and Hadfield services No.**67421** heads towards Glossop on the last leg of its journey. Soon to be displaced from duties such as these, the C13s could still be seen at London Road station on pilot duties-simmering away, dirty and unkempt. 67421 was withdrawn at the end of 1958. The last engine to go, No.67417, survived until January 1960.
B.K.B.Green

Approach to Glossop Station, January 10th.1961: An official photograph taken to show Bridge No.2-an underline bridge which led off Surrey Street, past the Glossop Borough Corporation stores yard and into a footpath which ran by Glossop Cricket Club's ground. Copious siding accommodation existed in the vicinity of Glossop Station: behind the camera Messrs.Olive & Partington, a local concern, had their own siding which ran alongside the Down line. A plentiful supply of logs can be seen behind the bridge parapet on the right-hand side. These would no doubt have belonged to Messrs.R.Goddard & Sons a local timber merchant on Surrey Street; the land adjacent to the railway here is designated "pole stacking ground" on a map dated 1954. As elsewhere, coal traffic was still handled at Glossop in those days. Beyond the signalbox, towards the station, were provided three sidings, two of which fed down into "coal shutes" (sic). The coal yard in question was off Surrey Street, just by its junction with Railway Street. Another timber yard, along with coal offices and the premises of Messrs.Abel Harrison Ltd., coal merchants, were sited here. Goods accommodation at Glossop was completed by a two-road goods warehouse with four cranes within and a 5-ton crane outside. Glossop's goods yard closed on June 14th.1966; the signalbox closed on October 6th.1968. Further rationalisation came on March 16th. the following year when the line from Glossop to Dinting was singled by removal of the Down line. *British Railways*

Glossop Central, n.d: Our old friend, C13 No.**67421**, stands in the platform with the return push-pull service to Manchester, London Road. The siding on the left served a cattle dock, though this is not shown as such on an official map dated 1954. To the right is the goods warehouse, a two-road affair mentioned previously. A mixture of trains served Glossop: some called at Dinting and continued down the branch before returning to Manchester. In contrast, some services travelled to Hadfield first, reversed and then called at Glossop. Others worked between Manchester and Sheffield, ventured down the branch from Dinting and then continued on their way to Sheffield-an arrangement which appears to have found particular favour on Sundays. The July 1938 timetable shows 17 regular weekday trains from Manchester to Glossop, a curiousity being the last train of the day (an 11.05 departure) from London Road which ran only on Tuesday, Thursday and Saturday-the latter being Glossop market day. The fastest run of the day from Manchester was without a doubt the 5.17 pm fromLondon Road which completed the journey in 26 minutes and called only at Mottram and Broadbottom and Dinting; the latter known in those days, incidentally, as "Glossop and Dinting." The 5.17- known unofficially as "The Glossop Express" survived the war and appears in the 1950 timetable, but by then an extra 4 minutes was allowed for the journey. *P. Ward*

Glossop Central, Summer 1953: Coronation Year, an event when the railways, still recovering from the effects of wartime, let their hair down somewhat with numerous celebratory titivations applied in the form of flags and bunting at various stations. The presence of the "overhead" is a reminder that this would be the last full year of steam working J11 0-6-0 No.**64311** has arrived at the terminus with a five-coach stopping service. The use of goods engines on passenger services here was not unusual, nor was it new; observations made pre-WWII show "Pom-Poms" (J11s) at work on trains from London Road to Hadfield and then back to Glossop. Glossop's "Central" suffix was dropped in 1974; the station becoming plain "Glossop" as and from May 6th.of that year. *N.E.Stead*

Glossop Branch, curve from Dinting South to East Junction 1954: The view round from the branch to the junction with the main line running east towards Hadfield. Overhead is bridge No.56 which carried Dinting Road over both the main line and the branch. This structure dated from 1884, the time of the re-modelling of the triangle and the doubling of the line to Glossop. Under the single arch of the bridge can be seen Home signals controlling the layout ahead: the arm on the left controlled entry to the Up Goods line (56 chains long) which ran from Dinting East Junction to Hadfield. That on the right controlled entry out onto the main line. The stylish low wooden structure, with looks akin to a miniature GCR signalbox, was a hut for the Signal and Telegraph Department (S&T). Notice the earth return bond for the "overhead" welded to the Bull-Head rail on the track nearest the camera. *B.K.B.Green*

Dinting East Junction, April 18th.1951: B1 4-6-0 crosses the junction with the Glossop branch and heads towards Dinting station with a Down express, possibly an excursion from former LMS territory-the headboard is coded "515". Steam will reign over Woodhead for more than three years yet, though preparations for electrification are well in hand. Steelwork for the "overhead" is in place and the newly-erected concrete posts are in situ alongside the Up line with supports ready to receive the 33kV feeder cables. Notice the bracket signals with the Distant for Mottram No.2 in a sagging position. Despite the introduction of some colour light signalling, the line was never re-signalled on an overall basis-something which militated against it when closure plans were first mooted. *Gordon Coltas*

Approach to Hadfield Station, n.d: A Class 506 EMU, with Motor Open Brake Second M59403M leading, approaches Hadfield-the limit of suburban electric working from Manchester. The scene is viewed from the Park Road overbridge; on the right can be seen the Goods line, installed by the LNER, which trails in to re-join the main line here from Dinting. In the right-hand background can be seen the sub-station once sited here-notice the high tension feeder cable running away from the lineside towards this. Fuller details of the electrification programme will appear in the subsequent volume. *W.A.Brown*

Hadfield Station, mid-1950s: Ancient and modern at Hadfield: a Class 506 EMU in the original dark green BR electric livery seen against the backdrop of the stone station buildings of SAuL&M vintage and the overbridge (Park Road, bridge No.58) with its semi-circular stone arches dating from 1844. The 1500v Dc units had a working life of just over 30 years, during which time the fortunes of the Woodhead line changed from that of a modernised, prestigious main line to a truncated stump. Trilbys, the odd cloth cap and raincoats were de rigeur when this picture was taken, to say nothing of smart suits for young ladies. And we musn't forget the little boy, cap on head and complete with white ankle socks-what a stark contrast to today's universal outfit of jeans and trainers! The signalbox on the far end of the platform was Hadfield West, sited a mere 836 yards from its neighbour, Hadfield East, up the line in the direction of Woodhead. *Harry Townley*

Hadfield for Hollingworth, c.1945: Hadfield station had opened in 1846, the suffix "for Hollingworth" was added later, but it is not known when. Hollingworth is a village some 1½ miles west of Hadfield itself, but such tongue-in-cheek descriptions never seemed to worry the railway companies! J11 No.**5324** is standing at the Up platform with a two-coach local working. The engine appears in the plain wartime black with the austere initials "NE" on the tender. (The 1946 number of 4437 was not applied to this engine until January 1946 which helps to date the picture). A 12-wheeled ex-GCR Saloon carriage with centre entrance door forms part of the two-coach formation. As BR No.65324, the engine depicted here was withdrawn in June 1962.

Collection of J.H.Turner

Hadfield Station, September 12th.1953: B1 No.**61153** sweeps through the station and tackles the 1-in-100 towards Valehouse with a Manchester-Marylebone Express. Interestingly, while expresses plying Manchester-London routes on the former LNWR and Midland lines always carried the legends "London-Manchester" on their carriage destination boards, those on the ex-GCR were always designated "Marylebone-Manchester"-preferring the name of the station to that of the Capital itself. The small waiting room building on the Down platform has architectural features reminiscent of those on the old Gorton station.

Gordon Coltas

Hadfield Station, October 11th.1953: The stone arches of the Park Road overbridge dominate the background as the ugly from of the Gresley Garratt No.**69999** pass through the station precincts. Precisely why the mammoth was being tried out over this section of the Woodhead line is obscure: the electrification was all but complete and steam working would be doomed within a twelvemonth. The monster had been converted to oil fring the previous year and following a hiatus was put through various tests. On this occasion it was booked to haul a load of about 600 tons (43 wagons) as far as Crowden. After a delay at Hadfield of some 25 minutes to raise steam, 69999 managed to get only as far as Torside Crossing before needing a further pause to regain its breath. The, then, "high-tec" electrification masts contrast with the oil and gas lamps. Careful observation of the lamp just ahead of the waiting room reveals the "Hadfield for Hollingworth" name still intact in the lamp glass. *B.K.B.Green*

Hadfield Station, n.d: A reverse view at Hadfield; this time we are looking towards Valehouse with the station footbridge and sidings ahead of us. The station footbridge, numbered 39, was reconstructed by the LNER circa 1935 using a secondhand structure. It was removed in March, 1971. By the footbridge steps a man clasps the hand of a child, a dog rummages behind while the duo watch the passage of a Bo-Bo electric, number unknown, pass through with a Down train of coal empties. A scene, quite humdrum yet so typical of the traffic pattern on this railway that had been set way back in the ninteenth century. *Harry Townley*

Hadfield West Signalbox, n.d: The interior of Hadfield West box, one of two signalboxes between Dinting and Valehouse. With hand on the accepting block from Hadfield East, in what is obviously a posed photograph, the signalman glances up at his track diagram. This, though drawn in the modern style, lacks any illuminated track circuit indicators, reliance being placed on the older type of moving bar instrument-seen just below the "Bobby's" wrist. Between the block instruments-of standard LNER pattern-is the box for "switching out" when the box was closed; then the block telegraph would be operable between the signalboxes on either side. Notice from the diagram the end of the loop from Dinting to this point, the layout of the goods yard and the rising gradient on the Up line towards Woodhead.
Glossop Heritage Centre Collection

Hadfield, looking East, 1960: A view from the east end of the Up platform looking towards Valehouse and Torside. Approaching on the Down line is a 6-coach express drawn by a, then, ubiquitous Co-Co electric locomotive. Goods facilities here were quite extensive, with facilities existing on both sides of the line. A warehouse building, with coal drops stood, out of sight, on the Up side; across on the Down was a through siding with an adjacent loop and shunting necks; exit was controlled by the two semaphore "dollies" on the right of the view. *L.M.Hobday*

Hadfield, February 3rd.1966: Certainly one of the less glamorous features of this part of the Woodhead line: the coal drops at Hadfield which stood alongside the Up line, east of the station, and were accessed from Station Road and Platt Street. Dow records that Hadfield's goods depot opened in 1845 and cost £895 to build, over three times that of nearby Broadbottom. Doubtless, the facilities shown here were resonsible for the much higher construction costs. Coal traffic had existed on the railways since the dawn of the system and the station goods yard with integral coal handling facilities was a feature of daily life almost everywhere. Coal drops such as these, though a feature in North-East England, were not common in the North-West. The onset of the use of modern fuels was reflected, inevitably, in a decline in coal traffic for both domestic and mill use. Notice the overhead equipment has been removed from the siding roads; records show this as being done, together with connections to the warehouse (seen in the background) on June 10th.1962. By this building can be seen the BR standard signalbox installed here some two years previously. As and from March 1st.1964 Hadfield East and West signalboxes had ceased to be block posts and the new box controlled all operations. Further decline in goods facilities here came about in 1968 when the warehouse sidings and the Down sidings Nos.2 & 3 were secured out of use. Looking rather out of place, a steam locomotive, possibly a Stanier 2-8-0, shrouded in steam shunts coal wagons in the Down sidings. *British Railways*

Hadfield East, n.d: A scene looking from bridge No.61 west towards Hadfield station and showing the exit from the goods yard and the Through Siding on the Down line, left-hand side. This vantage point, bridge No.61, is on the road from Tintwistle to the confusingly-named Padfield, a small village east of Hadfield on the south-east side of the line. A ex-LMS 3F 0-6-0 with a pick-up freight pulls out on to the Up main line having just left the Through Siding on the Down side. The distant chimneys and terraces of Hadfield are virtually the last remnants of civilisation before the vast stretches of open moorland that dwarf the railway and all but swallow it up on the long rising slog towards Woodhead. *Norman Jones*

Hadfield East, n.d: All is now moors, sky and water as we watch the 3F as it drifts beyond the Padfield Road bridge and edges cautiously towards signal HE3 awaiting the "right away" before moving off in the direction of Vale House. Hadfield East box can be seen on the right-hand side; the Down Goods line, a long lay-by siding, can be seen in the distance beyond the box. *Norman Jones*

Valehouse, August 1920: GCR Class 1 4-6-0 No.**423** *Sir Sam Fay* approaches Valehouse with the 2.15 p.m. Manchester London Road to Marylebone Express. Comprised of eleven corridor coaches the train is passing the Down Goods line and is approaching Valehouse signalbox. Goods or "Loop" lines, though the latter term is not used on the official track plans, were installed variously along the route to enable heavy, slow-moving coal trains to be held in between the passage of faster-moving traffic. The locomotive is tackling a rising gradient here of between 1-in-100 to 1-in-117. Several runaways were recorded in the days of loose-coupled, unbraked freight trains and the sand drag seen by the camera was installed for such contingencies. Of ¼ mile in length it extended from Valehouse signalbox in the direction of Hadfield East. Notice the points by the signal enabling detainees to be released back on to the running rails again. At the far end of the Goods line an Up train waits for a passage back onto the main line again. Just visible in the distance is the overbridge near Hadfield from where the pictures of the 3F were taken. *G.M.Shoults*

By Valehouse Signalbox, May 15th.1954: Class O4 No.**63850** passes Valehouse signalbox with an Up freight. Over twenty-four wagons are visible-more are outside the view of the camera-the front three appear to be loaded with scrap metal of some kind. Notice the Down Goods line to the left of the picture from where the photograph of No.423 was taken. In the background can be seen a part of the Valehouse reservoir, one of a series along the lineside here and constructed in the nineteenth century to meet the water supply needs of nearby Manchester. Valehouse reservoir was completed in July 1869. Of 63 acres in area, it was built with a maximum depth of 40 feet and was designed for a capacity of 343 million gallons of water. The name was taken from the hamlet of Vale House a place "amounting to some 600 souls" which was flooded to make the reservoir. Vale House Mills-engaged in the production of woollen cloth and cotton spinning were demolished and submerged. *A.C.Gilbert*

East of Valehouse, September 23rd.1946: A touch of post-War sparkle on a beautiful sunny Monday morning in the Pennine foothills. V2 No.**948**, looking clean and smart after re-numbering some three days earlier, is in charge of the 9.55 am Manchester to London express. The train has cleared Valehouse signalbox and is heading east up the 1-in-117 towards Torside and Crowden; the Up Goods line is in the background. The engine, then only just over four years old, is in the wartime unlined black livery and looks commendably clean as do the Gresley coaches in their classic LNER "varnished Teak" livery. Notice the gantries for the overhead catenary. These were erected before the war, work having been suspended on the outbreak of hostilities in 1939. During the war red lead protective paint had reportedly turned to pink after a while in the atmosphere. Fearing that such colours might attract enemy aircraft workmen were dispatched to paint the offending steelwork black! As part of the run-down of the line in its last years the Up Goods line was taken out of use on July 7th.1970. *J.D.Darby*

Valehouse, Up Goods Line, February 6th 1954: When selecting pictures showing motive power for publication a temptation exists to pick only those that show clean locomotives in spick and span condition. But photographs showing the real railway at work simply aren't like that. At best, the steam locomotive was a dirty beast requiring a lot of manual effort to maintain, clean and drive it. In the last years of British steam, freight locomotives in particular were seldom seen in pristine condition, something which by no means distracted from their enthusiastic following. Here, then, is such a machine: O4/3 No **63716** with steam leaking from the front end, slogging along the Up Goods line past Valehouse and climbing up the 1-in-117 ever nearer to the "hole" that was Woodhead Tunnel. Thirty-odd coal empties are strung behind the tender, the ensemble clanking and wheezing through the winter snows, a scene that must have been witnessed literally thousands of times at this same spot over the last hundred or more years-but soon to be no more. Notice the driver has his eye on the photographer wondering, perhaps, whatever possessed someone to venture out to this bleak spot in the depths of winter to photograph his train. What a hero!
B.K.B.Green

Valehouse, Down Main Line, February 6th 1954: Drifting down the 1-in-117, the fireman of O4/7 No **63876** will be having an easy time by comparison with his compatriots in the Up direction. Here, yet another trainload of Yorkshire coal drifts past the photographer and heads along the Down line in the direction of Hadfield and Godley. The wild, open and inhospitable nature of the terrain here is now apparent. A glance at a map of the area reveals the use of the word "Clough"-an old English word meaning a "ravine or narrow Glen" occurring repeatedly. "Small Clough", "Blackshaw Clough", "Ogden Clough" and in the background is Deepclough, the name being applied to the culvert over which the O4 has just traversed-past the colour light signal in the background. In 1907, when the loops ("Goods Lines") were being installed along here towards Crowden, considerable difficulty was experienced by underground streams saturating the peaty soil. Near to Crowden the line runs into a cutting and here a landslip occurred. In all, some 220,000 cubic yards of material were excavated in these works. Retaining walls and over twenty culverts were installed to cope with the problems.
B.K.B.Green

Torside, 1950s: At Torside the B6105 road from Glossop crossed the line via a level crossing-one of the very few on the route. Viewed from the footbridge, Bo-Bo No.**26022** is about to cross the roadway by the signalbox with an Up through freight train. Between the locomotive and the signalbox can be seen the Up Goods line which commenced at Vale House by milepost 14. Travelling from Torside in the Up direction towards Crowden, an effective four-track layout commenced just before milepost 15½ (just behind the camera) where a Down Goods line began; this was commissioned in October 1908. Four tracks continued through Crowden station where there was access to and from the main lines in both directions-all part of track alterations completed in 1908. The loops continued as far as Woodhead station, just past milepost 19 to finish just short of the tunnel mouth. More than one runaway freight train on the Down Goods line had ended up perilously close to the crossing-keeper's house seen in the bottom of the picture! *Norman Jones*

Torside Signalbox, n.d: A charming period view of the GCR-pattern signalbox at Torside, then known as "Torside Crossing." At least one signalman obviously had horticultural tendencies, not to say green fingers, as the splendid selection of potted plants below the windows shows. One of the men appearing in the photograph may well have been attached to a permanent way gang. Two such gangs, numbered 258 and of six men each, were based at Torside. Adding a final, quite wonderful, touch of human interest is the young girl clutching her pet dog at the bottom of the steps by the Up Goods line. This was quite probably the signalman's daughter who would have lived in the house opposite the box. A simple existence, an abundance of fresh air and wonderful scenery-only an endless procession of trains to punctuate the silence! Torside Reservoir, another Manchester Corporation entity and dating from 1864, can be seen in the background. *Glossop Heritage Centre collection*

Past Torside and the lonely crossing the Pennine main line continued its uphill climb at 1-in-117, a figure maintained almost the whole way up to the mouth of the Woodhead Tunnel itself. The vista now is one of moors, sky and water. Water, because this part of the valley, as touched on previously, was successively flooded by Manchester Corporation in the nineteenth century to provide a plentiful supply of clean water for the populace of their city. This ambitious programme of works was masterminded by the renowned Victorian water engineer John Frederick Bateman who acted as consulting engineer to the Manchester Corporation Waterworks. Bateman's reservoirs, constructed variously between 1848 and 1877, extended from Tintwistle, north-west of Glossop, to Woodhead. From a point beyond Hadfield the reservoirs, named Bottoms, Vale House, Hollingworth, Arnfield, Torside, Rhodeswood and Woodhead shadowed the alignment of the railway as the two fought the vagaries of nature to stake their claim for a place in this wild and inhospitable part of northern England.
At Crowden the old Chapel-en-le-Frith and Enterclough bridle turnpike road crossed an embankment which formed a dam between the two reservoirs of Torside and Woodhead. Some 100 yards east of this embankment lay, lonely and bleak, Crowden station-17 miles, 18 chains from Manchester London Road and opened by the MS&L on July 1st.1861.

Crowden, August 15th.1953: O4/3 No.**63716** passes light engine through the station on the Up Goods line. The tiny station "yard", just with a mere shunting neck, had obviously been used as a storage point for drums of cable in connection with the impending electrification programme. The familiar BICC drums resemble the much-loved Hornby 0 Gauge wagon load familiar to generations of youthful railway modellers. Through the vista of overhead electrical catenary the sinuous nature of the track layout here can be gauged. *Harry Townley*

Crowden Station, August 15th.1953: The ubiquitous B1 again: No.**61036** charges uphill towards Woodhead with an Up express. The view here gave the observer the impression of a four-track layout but, as mentioned previously, the outer tracks were goods lines-long loops commissioned here in 1908 to ease the traffic flow and forcing the rebuilding of the station. Across on the far side a string of wooden-bodied coal wagons, yet another trainload of Yorkshire coal for Lancashire and beyond, can be seen on the Down goods line. *Harry Townley*

Crowden Station, August 15th.1953: The photographer has positioned himself at the west end of the island platform to catch a V2, number unknown, at the head of a 10-coach express. The stock is a mixture of Gresley and Thompson vehicles, some in the British Railways carmine and cream livery, others still lingering in the so-called "varnished teak" finish of the LNER. There is a certain poignancy about this quite splendid view: this, Coronation Year, will be the last full year of steam operation over this rugged route, thus ending over a century of history. Notice the lone ex-MS&L 6-wheeled coach in the shunting neck. Dating from the 1870s or 1880s, this coach would almost certainly have travelled over Woodhead in its heyday. Now used as a static mess van, its days are over; who did it carry-perhaps past this very spot, day in, day out? History indeed. The crossovers exist to aid the movement of traffic from goods to main lines and vice-versa. A parallel arrangement existed at the opposite end of the platform. *Harry Townley*

Crowden Station, September 11th.1933: A Robinson 8K (LNER O4) - number unknown passes along the Down main line with a through freight train consisting, in part, of loco coal and uncut timber. The lofty GC - pattern semaphores clearly identify the territory. This picture gives a good view of the island platform layout here. Crowden station was rebuilt to this form between 1907 and 1908 when the Goods lines were installed from here through to Woodhead. Rationalisation of the track layout at Crowden was undertaken in 1967. The Up and Down Goods lines from Torside were taken out of use as and from Sunday, October 15th. 170 yards on the Woodhead side of Crowden signalbox, the Down Goods line was severed and formed trap points. The station footbridge, numbered 68 and spanning all four tracks, was removed in 1969. *E.R. Morten*

Crowden Station, c.1953: An unidentified 2-8-0 pulls away tender-first along the Up Goods line with a short train of empty wagons. The scene looks from the station footbridge towards Woodhead and shows the wild, open nature of the countryside in this spot. Going due north from this point the traveller would have to cover some eight miles of bleak, uninhabited moorland facing the rigours of Westend Moss, Tooleyshaw Moss-by Holme Moss (of TV transmitter fame)-and Wessenden Head Moor before alighting on the village of Slaithwaite across from the former LNWR Manchester to Huddersfield line. Crowden signalbox sits precariously above above the still, shining water of Woodhead reservoir.
H.B.Priestley

Crowden Station, August 15th.1953: A last look at this bleak outpost of the GCR main line as O4/7 No.**63750** drifts downhill along the Down Goods line with yet another trainload of coal from the Yorkshire pits. The mass of overhead electric wiring is a reminder that next year, 1954, will see an end to sights to such as this as the Woodhead line, to much acclaim, becomes Britain's first wholly electrified railway. Then Bo-Bo and Co-Co electrics with state-of-the-art regenerative braking will make silent ascents and descents of these moorland inclines with the same wagon loads of coal. Crowden Station closed on February 4th.1957.
Harry Townley

It is at Woodhead, a bleak and most remote spot in the midst of wild Pennine moorland, that the last part of the long climb eastwards began. On a gradient easing slightly, from 1-in-117 to 1-in-201, the all-pervading blackness of a 3 mile, 1 chain tunnel took trains from industrial Lancashire, through part of Derbyshire, then boring through sandstone and shale and into Yorkshire. The summit of the line, just short of Dunford Bridge station, was reached as trains emerged from the black hole that has become, in one way and another, the focus for this most fascinating stretch of railway.

Woodhead Station, June 6th.1938: A gaze down on the tiny station-looking away from the tunnel mouth along the Longdendale Valley. The two edifices seen in the picture, the castellated form of the station buildings and the Stationmaster's house on the left and the enormous water tank on the the Up platform, were massive structures. To the casual observer the platform buildings might have been thought of as being out of proportion to the station's importance. Woodhead, though, was seen as the "jewel in the crown" of a railway which was a triumph of Victorian engineering. In the distance can be seen the Goods lines which terminated here after a run of, in the case of the Up line, nearly four miles from Torside. Feintly visible, beyond the signal box, is the small goods yard; the Woodhead Stationmaster had the luxury of his own siding! Rambling through the middle of the scene is the Rver Etherow which cascaded down to fill Woodhead Reservoir. The river also received drainage water from the Woodhead Tunnel; Heyden Brook, another local watercourse, also fed the reservoir.
Collection of R.S.Carpenter

Woodhead Tunnel Mouth, n.d: The two tunnel portals at the western end viewed from the underbridge, No.70, over the River Etherow. Standing, monument-like, the left-hand, Up, tunnel is the later structure built between 1847 and 1852. Its identical twin, constructed between 1839 and 1845, which aroused so much Victorian indignation and outrage, stands over to the right. Massively solid-looking, the structures look as if they could withstand a thousand years use at this period in time. Yet, this was not to be so and within a fraction over the centenary of the first tunnel both structures had become life-expired-massive volumes of traffic having taken their toll. Drifting smoke suggests the recent passage of a train. The foul conditions in the tunnel are well-documented; in 1899 a signalbox was installed in the Up tunnel but was abandoned around 1909 due to the atrocious working conditions. Pneumatic signalling was installed in its place. To alleviate the suffocating atmosphere experienced by engine crews, not forgetting permanent way gangers, work on the ventilation shafts was carried out over the three years from 1912. Rather prosaically, the tunnels are listed in official records as Bridge (sic) No.70B. Observant readers who have followed my bridge numbers may be wondering where bridge No.70A went to. This number was allocated to a new River Etherow bridge which was constructed in 1953 towards completion of the new railway tunnel. The latter took the simple designation of Bridge 70C. *Author's collection*

Woodhead, August 17th.1947: O4/3 No.**3629**, one of the numerous Robinson GCR 8K 2-8-0s built for the ROD in 1917, emerges into the daylight from the Up tunnel. Observant readers may have picked up what looks like a "facing" crossover between the Up and Down lines. This is not so; the train is working "bang road"-wrong line to the layman. This was a Sunday when, frequently, one or the other tunnels would be the subject of a possession for repairs or inspection and single-line working, as here, would be in force. Notice one of the tunnel's ventilation shafts on the skyline alongside the overhead electric pylon. *D.L.Wilkinson*

Woodhead Station early 1950s: A fine panorama of Woodhead and the beautiful, wild expanse of land and water in the surrounding Longdendale Valley. These are exciting and busy times for the little station whose new 3-mile tunnel has become the focus for the biggest post-War civil engineering project on Britain's railways. On the Down platform demolition contractors are completing the job of removing the last remains of the Gothic station buildings. Plant packs the station yard as engineers are well on with the work of constructing a new bridge over the River Etherow which will form part of the re-aligned main line approaches to the new Woodhead tunnel. In the middle distance the Up Goods line can be seen terminating just by the signalbox; facing and trailing crossovers facilitate the movement of traffic in and out of the tunnel. The keen-eyed may be able to spot J11 No.**64344** making a cautious passage over the new bridge works. *J.D.Darby*

Woodhead Station, 1949: The start of a new era at Woodhead and one of the biggest post-War railway projects in the U.K. Set in the hillside along the side of the existing Down tunnel, work has just begun on the pilot tunnel for the new workings. Bored to dimensions of about one-fifth of the finished tunnel, the pilot tunnel was completed on May 16th.1951 when Mr.J.C.L.Train-member of the Railway Executive responsible for civil engineering-fired the shot to complete the break-through. With features from a past era of railway operation prominently displayed, an "Austerity" 2-8-0 drifts out of the tunnel with a Down through freight and crosses the River Etherow. A crew member hangs out of the cab gazing, no doubt, at the new works.
Reporter Group of Newspapers

Woodhead Station and Entrance to New Tunnel, May 30th 1954. An historic moment at Woodhead as Bo-Bo electric locomotives Nos.**26001** & **26016** run into the newly-commissioned Woodhead tunnel. This was the first time that electric locomotives had entered the tunnel under their own power. Forming a contrast to this, then, "state of the art" system B1 No.**61311** emerges "wrong line" out of the smoke-laden old Up tunnel with a Down express. Notice the re-aligned track formation to the new tunnel and the new station and stationmaster's house in the middle right-hand of the picture. Living conditions here must have improved drastically in the new building-forming a welcome contrast to the old house with its fortress-like, rather foreboding, appearance. New station buildings have been erected on the Down platform; the new signalbox stands out in the left-hand corner of the picture opposite the old water tank. *B.K.B.Green*

Woodhead, 1947: A group of railwaymen, doubtless all hardy fellows, taken by Benny Mc.Vey a Woodhead signalman outside the box. L to r are: Eric Bennet and Ken Birchenough, S&T Inspectors from Guide Bridge; Wilf Boardman district signalling inspector, Guide Bridge to Deepcar; Wilf Ward assistant mechanical lineman, Penistone; Colin Wray mechanical lineman, Penistone; George Fowler telegraph lineman, Penistone and Ted Bosnall a signalman at Woodhead who went to Hitchin to become a signalling inspector. *Benny Mc.Vey*

Woodhead, 1947: A picture taken looking east towards the tunnel, the Up Main with sand drag, Up Loop leading to the column tank road beneath the water tank, and Up platform can be seen to the left of the photograph. The Up Loop here was the last refuge before trains went into the notorious tunnel on a rising gradient. An unofficial practice by some drivers in steam days was for the engine of a train detained behind another in the loop to hook off and act as an impromptu banker for the train in front-thus giving a welcome shove up the ascending 1-in-117/201 towards the tunnel mouth. Once the "banker" had reached the tunnel mouth the driver would whistle to the train engine before halting and then reversing back to his own train. *Benny Mc.Vey*

Woodhead Station, 1947: One of the Woodhead signalmen hands the key token for single line working through the tunnel to the train engine (by the looks of things a new B1) of an Up express prior to entering the tunnel on a single line possession. Notice the sand drag beneath the first coach of the train and the castellated form of the station buildings in the distance. Woodhead signalbox had a 40-lever frame with a key token machine for single-line working through the tunnel in either up or down directions. In both the old tunnels there was a gong to warn drivers that they were approaching Distant signals. The gongs were attached to the lever arms of the signals concerned; the signal on the Up line was operated by Dunford Bridge box, that on the Down by Woodhead. *Benny Mc.Vey*

With this last glimpse of the old Woodhead tunnels we come to the end of the first part of our journey from Manchester London Road to Sheffield. The second part of this work will take a detailed look at the line from the eastern side of the tunnel, at Dunford Bridge, will continue via Penistone and in to Victoria Station. Special attention has been paid to the electrification of the line as well as the inclusion of many previously unpublished photographs of steam locomotives at work over this most historic railway.

Woodhead Down Tunnel mouth, n.d: The view that must have been seen by countless thousands of footplate crews over around a hundred years as their charges and trains rolled out of the three mile tunnel and began the long descent towards Manchester. Caught neatly in the "keyhole" frame is the Etherow bridge and the Gothic form of Woodhead Station and the adjacent Stationmaster's house. *David Ibbotson*